Praise for *The Nir*

This is a very well researched an
dia of leaders and leadership. A must-read for all current and
aspiring leaders. DAME CILLA SNOWBALL, WELLCOME TRUST
GOVERNOR, GREAT PRIVATE SECTOR COUNCIL CHAIR AND
FORMER GROUP CEO AND GROUP CHAIRMAN OF AMV BBDO

Every successful business is the result of successful leadership.
However, there are wildly different types of leaders, with different strategies. Different markets, organizational cultures and
industries require different leadership. And your own abilities
and style determine your own leadership. James Ashton has
produced a fresh, thoughtful, modern look at business leadership
that will provide key insight to leaderships everywhere. REID
HOFFMAN, LINKEDIN CO-FOUNDER, AUTHOR OF *BLITZSCALING*
AND HOST OF *MASTERS OF SCALE* PODCAST

I've always said life is 50 per cent luck and 50 per cent what you
do with it. James Ashton's *The Nine Types of Leader* captures the
luck and actions of CEOs around the world, and then turns it into
an opportunity for you to look at what you've been given and use
it to shape the leader you will become. AJAY BANGA, MASTERCARD
EXECUTIVE CHAIRMAN

From interviews with a who's who of global business glitterati,
James Ashton's new breakdown of nine types of leader is
purposeful, authentic and delivered with his trademark readabil-
ity. STEVIE SPRING, CHAIRMAN OF THE BRITISH COUNCIL AND
THE MENTAL HEALTH CHARITY MIND

James Ashton has managed to produce a book about leadership
that stands out in a busy field and cuts through management
waffle. Pin-sharp analysis of the different types of leader,
insightful commentary about the many leadership personalities
he has interviewed over the years and vivid storytelling. As you
read, you can't help but think about the type of leader you are

yourself (and secretly hope it's the Human one). A great read – thoroughly enjoyed it. RITA CLIFTON, CBE, PORTFOLIO CHAIR, NON-EXECUTIVE DIRECTOR AND AUTHOR OF *LOVE YOUR IMPOSTER*

Business leaders are peculiar and brave. Few aspire to it; even fewer succeed. James Ashton has shrewdly tabulated his own butterfly collection of this exotic breed. Long on narrative, short on jargon and very entertaining. SIR PETER BAZALGETTE, ITV CHAIRMAN AND FORMER CHAIR OF ARTS COUNCIL ENGLAND

James Ashton has a knack for unpicking how leaders' motivations and methods develop over many years. This book neatly compiles a range of different approaches and suggests where leadership goes next as modern corporations and stakeholder demands evolve. GAVIN PATTERSON, SALESFORCE PRESIDENT AND CHIEF REVENUE OFFICER AND FORMER CHIEF EXECUTIVE OF BT GROUP

The world needs more great leaders, and James Ashton's thoughtful taxonomy points the way towards better leadership. Career-minded executives should pick it up. DAMBISA MOYO, GLOBAL ECONO-MIST, AUTHOR, 3M AND CHEVRON BOARD DIRECTOR AND FORMER BOARD DIRECTOR OF BARRICK GOLD AND BARCLAYS

Packed full of fascinating real-world examples of the leaders that James Ashton has spent years researching and interviewing, this entertaining book shows how the different personality traits of leadership can play out in the human beings running some of our biggest businesses. CHRIS HIRST, HAVAS CREATIVE GLOBAL NETWORK CHIEF EXECUTIVE AND AUTHOR OF *NO BULLSH*T LEADERSHIP*

A very readable book about the types of modern business leadership, sprinkled with great personal anecdotes and inside stories. If you only buy one book on leadership this year, make it this one! BRIAN MCBRIDE, TRAINLINE CHAIRMAN, STANDARD LIFE ABERDEEN, WIGGLE AND KINNEVIK NON-EXECUTIVE DIRECTOR, FORMER CHAIRMAN OF ASOS AND FORMER CHIEF EXECUTIVE OF AMAZON.CO.UK

A timely book – definitely one for the Davos crowd. SARAH SANDS, FORMER BBC RADIO 4 TODAY PROGRAMME EDITOR AND FORMER *EVENING STANDARD* EDITOR

The Nine Types of Leader

How the leaders of tomorrow can learn from the leaders of today

James Ashton

KoganPage

Publisher's note

Every possible effort has been made to ensure that the information contained in this book is accurate at the time of going to press, and the publishers and authors cannot accept responsibility for any errors or omissions, however caused. No responsibility for loss or damage occasioned to any person acting, or refraining from action, as a result of the material in this publication can be accepted by the editor, the publisher or the author.

First published in Great Britain and the United States in 2021 by Kogan Page Limited

2nd Floor, 45 Gee Street
London
EC1V 3RS
United Kingdom

122 W 27th St, 10th Floor
New York, NY 10001
USA

4737/23 Ansari Road
Daryaganj
New Delhi 110002
India

www.koganpage.com

Kogan Page books are printed on paper from sustainable forests.

© James Ashton, 2021

The right of James Ashton to be identified as the author of this work has been asserted by him in accordance with the Copyright, Designs and Patents Act 1988.

ISBNs

Hardback	978 1 78966 698 4
Paperback	978 1 78966 696 0
Ebook	978 1 78966 697 7
Audiobook	978 1 78966 796 7

British Library Cataloguing-in-Publication Data

A CIP record for this book is available from the British Library.

Library of Congress Cataloging-in-Publication Data

Names: Ashton, James (Journalist) author.
Title: The nine types of leader: how the leaders of tomorrow can learn
  from the leaders of today / James Ashton.
Description: 1st Edition. | New York: Kogan Page Inc, 2021. | Includes
  bibliographical references and index.
Identifiers: LCCN 2020044132 (print) | LCCN 2020044133 (ebook) | ISBN
  9781789666984 (hardback) | ISBN 9781789666960 (paperback) | ISBN
  9781789666977 (ebook)
Subjects: LCSH: Executives–Psychology. | Leadership. | Management.
Classification: LCC HD38.2 .A754 2021 (print) | LCC HD38.2 (ebook) | DDC
  658.4/092–dc23
LC record available at https://lccn.loc.gov/2020044132
LC ebook record available at https://lccn.loc.gov/2020044133

Typeset by Integra Software Services Pondicherry
Print production managed by Jellyfish
Printed and bound by 4edge Limited, UK

To Viveka and Alice, my greatest supporters,
and to Oscar, who is always with us.

Contents

Prologue

When I set out to write this book, I was determined not to produce another academic study of leadership. Much ink has been spilt on plenty of those, written by greater minds than mine. And besides, rather than combing through balance sheets or charts or board papers or decades of management theory to come up with something new and inspiring, my primary source material is – largely – all my own work.

Over more than 20 years of journalism I have accrued hours and hours in the company of chief executives. Sometimes fleetingly, for the best part of an hour across a boardroom table, in a recording studio or on a conference stage; sometimes socially too, getting to know them gradually over a long period at parties, breakfasts and dinners that oil corporate life in London and beyond. I hope it adds up to a detailed understanding of what makes the boss class tick, their ambitions and fears, how they got where they are – and how they stay there.

In journalism, the power lies in opinion. It is why the populist Fox News thrived in the United States even before the Trump era and the divisive topic of Brexit left the BBC somewhat tongue-tied in its pursuit of editorial balance. Newspapers are viewspapers in which columnists hold sway, purveying thought-provoking, sometimes pungent views from beneath statesmanlike picture bylines. I like writing those too but must admit I have always loved conducting interviews, where the subject must obviously be the star and granted sufficient oxygen to speak.

Very early on in my career I remember journeying up to glamour-free Luton to the north of London to interview Sir Stelios Haji-Ioannou, his workspace a tiny perch at the end of a table in an aircraft hangar from where he masterminded the European expansion of the budget airline easyJet and was now turning his attention to other ventures. Another formative encounter was with Howard Schultz, the Starbucks tycoon, soon after he acquired the Seattle Coffee Company that gave the chain a bridgehead into the UK. Schultz appeared captive that day in a large armchair at the back of one of his coffee outlets as a production line of journalists processed past. It got me thinking about the nature of business, what drives the leaders behind these brands, and why they wanted to tell me about it.

Sports journalists have their star strikers and Olympic athletes, political writers obsess over the activities of ministers, senators, heads of state and the ideas of policy wonks. For me it has always been a fascination with chief executives, those leaders of giant workforces – often larger than a stadium full of fans or a country's population – that generate great wealth, steward famous brand names or vital causes.

I soon understood my role. If I didn't ask the question I wanted answering then nobody would. At the age of 18, in a late-night interview conducted for my local hospital radio station in West Yorkshire, I still regret not having the bravado to ask the comedian Sir Ken Dodd about his tax affairs when I had the chance. More bite was needed – and more preparation. Several years later, I resolved never to show up as unready as a journalist with whom I shared a slot for a joint interview – itself a disastrous format. His opening gambit to the chief executive across the table was: 'So, what do you do?', which is the sort of small talk entrée you might expect the British royal family to trot out.

The joy of an interview comes in three stages. There is the before: pulling apart a beautifully botoxed CV, plump with superlatives and vaunting achievement that, together with a read-around and a ring-around, acts as a useful guide to where the real story lies. There is the after: crafting 1,300 or so words that sum up the subject, with some emphasis on finding a colourful three-paragraph drop intro to entice readers in. It is the meat in the sandwich I enjoy most: part conversation, part joust. The sights, the sounds, the figuring out: where am I, who is this person, why do they deserve to feature in my publication?

Efforts to sanitize the modern press interview have made great progress. These summit meetings are conceived to take place in bland rooms with heavily supervised chief executives offering up bland answers decorated with management speak, acronyms and key messages. And yes, sometimes they are so predictable that some write-ups could be produced before actual contact is made. The journalist is left to feel complicit in a set piece, a carefully choreographed decoration of an illustrious executive career.

But only sometimes. The barricades erected by corporate imagemakers are an invitation to delve deeper and press harder, to ditch the bland in favour of the chinks of light shone on a leader's motivations and upbringing. Rather than a narrow prism, an interview properly handled is an opportunity to discover plenty about an individual's accumulated experience, through their answers but also through their body language, the location, even the time of day. The bosses who gamely turned up at my office wanted to be helpful or needed a favour; the leader who reluctantly assented to a chat during a noisy awards dinner that sent my Dictaphone into overdrive clearly didn't give a damn. Only once have I had to call back for a follow-up chat when I realized too late that a leader had beaten me. As it stood, he was just too boring to commit to print.

Many chief executives opt not to put themselves through the ordeal. For some, media relations activity is all risk, no reward. How presumptuous to be plastered across a full page, adorned with a portrait photo. How fatuous to contribute to a sidebar detailing their favourite movie, particular family relationships, leisure pursuits and what they had for breakfast.

Such a mindset suggests that the interviews I have collected must put across a lop-sided view of leadership. Rather than a broad spread of bosses, here is a subset of the most talkative, egotistical or pliant.

Certainly, media exposure is no corollary of success. Some terrible chief executives talk themselves up in the hope of polishing their legacy, while many good ones choose to say nothing. 'It's not about me, I'm just part of the team,' is a familiar but specious excuse for not finding the time in their hectic diary to engage.

Of course, those leaders that play the game want to push their cause. They might also want to correct misapprehensions, project a particular image, contribute to the national conversation or – as I have often found to be the case even in these ultra-cautious times – agree to be interviewed simply because they have been asked.

Rather than being out-and-out self-promoters – although some surely are – these are the enlightened ranks of the boss class. They understand that communication is a key part of leadership, whether running a tiny, low-profile widget maker or a world-famous corporation like Coca-Cola. Giving an interview is to offer out the chance to have your performance, personality and leadership style scrutinized. The three are inextricably linked.

Such scrutiny can be done at a distance by studying the familiar corporate metrics – underlying earnings, return on equity, total shareholder return, carbon footprint, customer and staff satisfaction – or gathering views from shareholders and former colleagues. City analysts, academics and historians cover much of this territory. Similarly, chief executives can transmit their thoughts directly to staff or the wider world via social media or company intranet without the risk of being misinterpreted.

But that route fails to recognize what a rigorous media still offers. At a time when authenticity is perhaps the most prized leadership attribute, here is a credibility filter that rewards success, combats mistrust, highlights challenges and shows up fakers and failures, often in their own words. That drive for keeping it real could be why up-close, unstructured, sometimes unguarded media such as podcasting is riding high. It is another test to be put through, like a job interview with no appointment at the end.

There are only nine types

After 400 such encounters from San Francisco to Stockholm and Singapore, in boardrooms, hotel lobbies, over breakfast, lunch and dinner and in planes, trains and automobiles, I have found these interviews to be the perfect vantage point from which to identify and analyse the Nine Types of Leader.

I interviewed so many chief executives, chairmen and similar that I began to see patterns in the crowd wisdom. Not only in how leaders answered my questions – that was down to the cookie-cutter media training some of them had been given – but in their approach to business and life. I wanted to see if I could group them together like signs of the zodiac or the Happy Families card game. For some leaders it was obvious, but some had a blend of ability, style and background. Others changed and developed during their career.

For this book I have looked back and studied numerous interviews from the last 20 years and refreshed some with follow-up conversations. I conducted many more anew, wrote in further examples with similar backgrounds or patterns of behaviour, and borrowed excerpts from my leadership podcast. Also included are leaders of not-for-profit organizations who are rarely credited for facing many of the same challenges as their corporate cousins. The criterion for inclusion is gloriously subjective: I think their take on life and business fits one of my nine types. If a business leader has had a colourful career, all the better.

I am sometimes asked what my best interview has been so far. If I answer based on who the interviewee was, that might be Facebook's Sheryl Sandberg, Sir Richard Branson or Carl-Henric Svanberg just as he arrived as chairman of BP, one of the prime roles in UK business. If I judge based on what was said, I would go for Tesco's Dave Lewis, TED's Chris Anderson or the newspaper proprietor

Richard Desmond, bored and blunt before he alighted on his acquisition of UK broadcaster Channel 5.

But the purpose of this book is to assess who are the best leaders. It quickly became clear to me there are some excellent, inspirational bosses but equally there are some who do not deserve to have been put in positions of great power. A third category is those poorly matched to their roles.

For would-be leaders this book is a guide to help identify who you are and how you can improve performance. It assesses the strengths and weaknesses of each leadership type and where and when they are best deployed. And, as the world seeks to recover from the 2020 Covid-19 pandemic – the most acute test of leadership in living memory – it projects how future leaders can learn from what has gone before.

By the way, 'What kind of leader are you?' is a question guaranteed to evince a seat-squirming answer every time. The truth is leaders rarely like to put it into words for external consumption; sometimes they don't know. And even if they do, their chosen approach to leadership is not necessarily how it comes over. Perhaps this book will help them answer better.

Acknowledgements

I couldn't have written this book without the opportunities a career in financial journalism has presented. Many of the interviews I reference here were published in newspapers I have had the pleasure to work for and contribute to over many years, including the *Evening Standard*, the *Independent* titles, *Daily* and *Sunday Telegraph*, *The Times* and *The Sunday Times*, *Daily Mail* and *Mail on Sunday*.

Thanks to colleagues from whom I have learnt much and who continue to produce deft, incisive and entertaining work day in, day out despite the industry's tough economics. To anyone that has read this far, please buy a newspaper – regularly.

The idea for this book simmered for several years while other projects came to the boil. I am indebted to several people who encouraged me to just get on with it: Rita Clifton, Justine Solomons and Dambisa Moyo. Alex Brummer told me once to 'write what you know' which is always a good place to start.

Thanks to the many CEOs who went back over their careers with me and shared their leadership thinking. Wise counsel from Martin Scicluna, Brian McBride, Paul Geddes and John Ainley improved the text markedly. There were vital introductions made by Julia Hobsbawm and Rick Haythornthwaite and Andrew Kakabadse and Stefan Stern were generous in reading and critiquing draft chapters.

Toby Mundy and his team at Aevitas Creative road-tested my ideas before I pressed 'send' and helped me to decide that nine was the magic number.

Chris Cudmore and his team at Kogan Page showed great professional dedication during a pandemic to ensure publication remained on track.

Moving closer to home... Mum and Dad: isn't it remarkable how far the *Huddersfield Daily Examiner*'s junior journalist competition will take you?

And finally, for their endless love and support: Viveka, Alice and Oscar, who is always with us.

Introduction

Meet the boss class

Early evening on the third Monday in May, when London weather is still straining to shake off the last chills of spring, a queue snakes along Chelsea Embankment. Heavy with grey suits and grey hair, shuffling forward two-by-two alongside iron barriers, this is a crowd not used to waiting in line.

Enlivened by flashes of floral pattern, smiles and waves, with many grimly clutching furled umbrellas just in case, here are Britain's business elite and their partners at play.

Year after year, the gala preview of the Chelsea Flower Show is a magnet that draws UK corporate might together in one place for a couple of hours like no other date in the diary.

Soon after the Queen has inspected the blooms and departed, champagne is poured, canapes plated and the networking begins. In they flock through Royal Hospital Chelsea's Thames Gate: FTSE 100 chief executives, chairmen, headhunters, funds chiefs, senior politicians, newspaper editors and public relations gurus. All come as guests of the investment banks, asset managers and accounting firms which typically sponsor the horticultural displays shown off as the starting gun fires on London's summer season of corporate hospitality.

Portrayed outside the business pages or specialist broadcast bulletins, these leaders are regularly regarded as either out-for-themselves villains or soaring superheroes. The former image is coloured by the after-effects of the 2008 financial crisis that cast a long shadow of economic disparity; the latter because of the idolatry of entrepreneurs, innovators and the handful that punch through into the public consciousness for doing good while doing well. These stereotypes are reinforced by business dealings reimagined as entertainment, whether it is the cut-throat conflict or risk taking as seen on *The Apprentice*, *Shark Tank* or *Dragons' Den*.

In truth, all life is here. Anyone interested in the reality of the world of big business and finance should mount a Sir David Attenborough-like study of the species at Chelsea. They won't discover many toiling small business owners whose enterprises make up the grass roots of the UK economy. Instead, on show here are London's captains of industry, who sit atop big, international employers and well-known brands. There are similar 'soft' summits that take place all over the world, at conferences and blue riband sporting fixtures.

Where chief executives lead, thousands follow. They are a community that powers global prosperity more than politicians or regulators can ever hope. This exclusive club – there is, by definition, only one per company – make the final call on strategy that supports jobs and investment to drive corporate growth and shareholder returns.

Yet their impact is far greater than merely numbers on a balance sheet or staff stationed along the production line. They must also set the tone and culture of their multi-billion-pound organization and sometimes an entire industry. These companies have changed immeasurably over time. Many count intangible assets, not fleets of plant and machinery, as an indicator of wealth. Technology means they are not boxed in by national borders. But they all still need someone with whom the buck stops. Whether they like it or not, business leaders are the always-on figure-heads that serve as a lightning rod for attacks and recipient of plaudits alike.

It appears to be a charmed life. On the one hand, they are phenomenally well-paid Masters of the Universe, cossetted more than ever by diary secretaries and image consultants that manage their lives. The highest-powered have limousine drivers and private jets at their disposal to shuttle them from meeting to meeting across the globe. When something goes wrong, they can often blame it on events outside their control.

However, just as many have their feet on the ground as head in the skies, catching the train to work instead of being ferried to check-in. And the job has undoubtedly become harder in the last decade. Even the title shows the stakes have been raised: from managing director to chief executive to leader in a few short years. Expectations are sky-high when billions of dollars of investment are at stake.

It is hard to believe that one man or woman can single-handedly make a big difference to outcomes. Yet they are paid to do precisely that. Chief executives must manage numerous stakeholders: investors, staff, suppliers and the wider community. They must balance demands for short-term performance with long-term vision. They must prepare for a technology-powered future that features nimble start-up competitors eager to rip up the old corporate order. And they do all this against a backdrop of unpredictable political and economic environments and a fast-spinning news cycle, where reputations can be shredded in minutes. No wonder they work so hard to find time to think.

'I optimize my life for the work I have and whatever information I need I get people to help me,' said Hans Vestberg, who received book summaries from his staff to save him time while he served as chief executive of Swedish telecoms equipment maker Ericsson for six years until 2016.[1] He was appointed to lead Verizon Communications, the US telecoms giant, in 2018.

Also in the chief executive's in-tray is the fact that public trust in big business remains stubbornly low. Leaders must parry boardroom pressures but remain cognisant of life outside. Despite great efforts, the jury is out on the role of business as a force for good in society. The positive initiatives of the many are often cancelled out by a malign few. And around the flashpoint of remuneration, it seems the divide will never be breached.

Much unites them. First of all – and at a superficial level – appearances. Image matters. Chief executives are well-dressed, with good teeth, gleaming eyes, quick wit and healthy glow. They can afford to be. They are also, by turns, keen to gossip, firm but fair, eager to champion their virtues, accentuate the positive, put on a brave face when times are tough and offer a little help or advice when required. But good grooming and user friendliness did not get them where they are today.

They exude confidence in their own ability. They can be arrogant. They probably don't listen enough. They take too long to correct mistakes. They don't set out to fail. They are unusually competitive and have a desire to dominate. Yet that inherent passion can be buried from view. The question of how they got where they are is often batted away – it wasn't a conscious thing, honestly.

However, to have reached a career pinnacle that puts them on the guest list to stroll around Chelsea did not happen without years of hard work, family sacrifice and a forgiving partner. There will have been luck too: a chance to shine that presented itself early when they professed they were not ready, a fortuitous overseas posting that fast-forwarded their career, or a keen mentor who pushed them on beyond the treacle layer of middle management.

The most common trait shared by those processing through the narrow funnel of Thames Gate is success. They must have impressed their peers and superiors on the way up to get a chance to lead. They must have found the right blend of skills and personality to inspire people to follow them – at board level, on the shop floor and maybe even in broader society. Over time they must have learnt to assemble and enable an impressive team, not just control its members.

Beyond these broad brushstrokes, this book will show that how chief executives come to lead is a diverse career showcase. So too is how they choose to lead, following one of nine distinct types, shaped by their early experience, training, the organization they find themselves in – or sometimes even by birth.

Pushing ahead

Some started out selling soap powder or headache pills at consumer goods giants such as Procter & Gamble or Reckitt Benckiser. Others spent their twenties finding their way around audits, restructurings or consulting projects at one of the Big Four professional services firms or fast-tracking through McKinsey or Goldman Sachs after studying philosophy, politics and economics at Oxford or Cambridge. Chances are they will have burnished their credentials with a mid-career MBA or stint at Harvard or similar illustrious seat of learning.

There appears to be a handful of prescribed routes to the top for business leaders, typically through one of the talent factories famous for turning out future chief executives with an all-round grounding.

There are exceptions of course. Two leadership types I spend a chapter on, Founders and Scions, are effectively talent-spotted by themselves or their families. But even they are likely to have served an apprenticeship somewhere to learn the ropes of how a large firm operates.

There are techniques for getting in and then getting on by propelling themselves up through an organization.

Then, like a high-stakes card game, future leaders must decide whether to stick or twist – hang on for a shot at high office or quit for another opportunity at a rival company. And when they get to the top, they must act like the boss, keeping their feet on the ground at the same time as realizing that colleagues will never want to simply shoot the breeze with them again.

My very subjective analysis suggests that roughly half of corporate leaders are long servers who have spent little or no time working elsewhere on their way to becoming the boss. These include three more types: the Alphas, who have assiduously built a power base over a long period; Diplomats, where longevity is often a requirement for leading; and Lovers, who wouldn't dream of doing anything else other than what they are already doing.

On the other hand, three further leadership types – Sellers, Campaigners and Fixers – are more likely to have played the field, assembling a range of experience from roles of ascending seniority at several employers before landing the first of their top jobs that closely match their skillset. Finally, I pull together the attributes I think will combine to create the effective leaders of the future, the experimental, digitally savvy bosses who are christened here as Humans.

A leader's career trajectory begins before they know it. Simply being born a privileged white male shortens the odds on them making progress. In the UK, much effort has been made to introduce blind CV recruitment that restricts bias against women, ethnic minorities and the working classes. Employers hire by key skills instead of academic attainment and have widened their outreach to a broader range of schools. Those efforts may impact the next generation of leaders, but for now 'good' schools and Russell Group universities dominate leaders' CVs.

There is evidence the UK has become more meritocratic, according to board adviser and executive coach John Ainley, especially compared to Germany or to France, with its system of Grandes Écoles and two leading French business schools, HEC Paris (Hautes Études Commerciales de Paris) and INSEAD, through which numerous business leaders pass.

Of course, few in their twenties are striving for the top with a genuine understanding of how to get there. As a graduate looking for his first job in India 40 years ago, Ajay Banga, the future leader of financial services group Mastercard, only set out to work for a company that was 'good and global'. That turned out to be the consumer goods giant Nestlé.

However, there are early signs of leaders-in-waiting, if not from their education path, then perhaps from formative entrepreneurial flourishes. That might just be a willingness to earn money as a teenager, or a small business they got going at university. The BBC's director-general Tim Davie and John Vincent, co-founder of healthy fast-food chain Leon, fall into this category.

In fact, multiple life experiences shape leaders, like all of us. The early death of a parent or coping with dyslexia is a familiar occurrence among Founders, who must be determined to succeed. As one of only a handful of girls studying at Culford School in Bury St Edmonds, Dame Jayne-Anne Gadhia was unknowingly prepared for the masculine world of banking years before she led the challenger bank Virgin Money onto the stock market.

Future leaders must have personal drive and an appetite for hard work. Mark Cutifani, the chief executive of diversified mining giant Anglo American, which owns diamond retailer De Beers, raced through his engineering degree at Wollongong University in New South Wales while working night shifts in a mine.

And serendipity plays a part. Richard Houston, the senior partner and chief executive of Deloitte in 13 countries across Europe, might have followed his father into science if meeting his future wife had not put him off from studying at the Massachusetts Institute of Technology for a year. But he also fancied a career that was 'people-based' and not stuck behind a laboratory bench, a desire that eventually took him into consulting.

Most importantly, what future leaders have to offer must tally with what corporations are looking for. The general business experience required to propel them into the chief executive's seat can come later. Recruiters are desperate to vary their graduate intake, signing up standout candidates that don't necessarily impress with top-of-the-class academic excellence so much as quick wits, creativity and something that marks a departure from the norm.

One former Goldman Sachs recruiter, writing anonymously, said that the investment bank hunted out history and literature graduates to diversify the ranks of its new starters away from the purely financial. More tellingly, he or she disclosed that Goldman looked for ambition in its recruits, a hard-to-quantify quality but surely found in the high number of competitive sports people it has taken on.[2]

In its halcyon days, Procter & Gamble lured graduates with entrepreneurial backgrounds into its popular sales and marketing programmes. There was no mention of soap powder or shampoo in its own marketing materials though. One memorable campaign promised applicants: 'We will teach you how to run a business at 25.'

Corporations try to champion continuous improvement and that means hunting for hires unafraid to challenge their superiors. The digital giant Amazon uses 'bar raisers' in its hiring process.[3] These are third-party interviewers brought in to assess candidates precisely because they are not associated with in-house teams and therefore are stripped of prejudice. The name is a reminder that each hire should be better than 50 per cent of those currently in similar roles. On its website Amazon lists 14 leadership techniques it is looking for, including an expectation that recruits will take great ownership, keep learning and think big. 'Leaders are obligated to respectfully challenge decisions when they disagree, even when doing so is uncomfortable or exhausting,' it states.[4]

That ability is not far from what McKinsey has been demanding of its staff for years. Its 'obligation to dissent' was a core principle first expressed by one of the management consultancy's founding partners, Marvin Bower, who understood that disagreement – without wrecking professional relationships – was a powerful tool.[5]

Raw materials

The right raw materials are important to work with – but so is the willingness to pick up more. 'I learnt very early on that I had to learn,' said David Sproul, Houston's predecessor at the helm of Deloitte.[6] Marked out as a highflier at 30 when he made partner, he was brought down to earth with a bump when the first team awayday he led ended in disaster.

Learning from the best at close quarters can be vital. The chairman of Inter Ikea since 2016, Anders Dahlvig was the personal assistant to Ikea founder Ingvar Kamprad early in his career, while the London Stock Exchange's chief executive David Schwimmer was chief of staff to Lloyd Blankfein during his 20-year rise at Goldman Sachs. Dara Khosrowshahi, the chief executive of ride-hailing app Uber, owes his leadership career to tech investor Barry Diller, who parachuted him in to lead travel website Expedia in 2005 after previously hiring the media banker to work for him. Like Scions without the bloodline, this exposure can turbocharge progress without encumbering rising stars with the weight of history.

Another positive attribute is formative failure. 'If you have a chance to work in a business which doesn't work out you will actually learn more probably than you ever learn from some of your more successful experiences,' said Evelyn Bourke, recounting efforts to build an Italian financial advice firm early in her career.[7] In 2016 Bourke become chief executive of Bupa, the private healthcare insurer and provider to 33 million customers in major markets including Australia, Spain and the UK.

The key skill of leading people, essential as future leaders scale the organization, is often – ironically – picked up away from the coalface. Business school is falling out of favour, especially among self-made technology entrepreneurs. But it remains a calling card that reassures recruiters when they see it on a CV because as well as teaching due process through case studies, it covers softer skills. They can often get squeezed out by busy people who might have disregarded how they relate to those around them in the day-to-day rush to do the job.

The boardroom pull

Few company announcements take more preparation than the unveiling of a new chief executive. In the days before, much effort goes into how the new leader will be unveiled so they land well with shareholders and staff. In the months prior to that, the job is likely to be to communicate the departure of the predecessor without a loss of confidence or goodwill. But for most well-drilled companies, that early morning statement to the stock exchange – assuming they are publicly listed – is the result of a continuous process that could go back years.

Any large firm has a talent plan at the top. At all times an heir apparent is identified as an insurance policy in case the incumbent chief executive leaves in a hurry or is incapacitated. If the boss gets hit by a bus, no company starts from scratch in the race to replace him or her.

Lower down, the top 300 managers, say, are involved in broader succession planning so that the best prospects are always learning and being stretched. It is a reminder that for all would-be leaders to push themselves up through an organization, there needs to be significant pull from above for them to achieve their ultimate goal. That depends on the assessment of two factors: skills and personality.

Choosing an organization's next chief executive is a decision for the board, backed up by at least one external adviser such as a headhunting firm and sometimes canvassing the opinions of shareholders. The ideal situation is to have a strong internal candidate to test against who is available on the external market, according to Brian McBride, the Amazon, T-Mobile and ASOS boardroom veteran who has been involved in numerous appointments. But it depends on the status of the company. The chairman and fellow directors are influenced by what type of leadership is required today but are also focused on future challenges they think will emerge.

Sometimes a leading internal candidate is worthy and capable on paper and the safest choice but he or she might not fit the bill if the organization needs a shake-up. An external candidate who has moved around during their career shows adaptability and brings fresh ideas but there is risk attached.

The choice starts with their CV. Internal candidates tend to emerge from a handful of divisions, such as finance or marketing. Most important is that they understand process, which is a way of saying they know how all the moving parts of a business work. That breadth crossed with industry experience is very attractive.

Externally, recruiters look for industry relevance as the starting point, without the requirement of expert knowledge. More valuable is IQ – intelligence quotient – a measure of cleverness, worldliness and the pace at which they can learn. Leaders should be smart.

Pretty quickly EQ – emotional intelligence – becomes an equally important factor. That covers interpersonal skills, charisma, how they lead and how that fits the culture of the organization. An enlightened chairman will take background soundings before a candidate gets anywhere near the shortlist. If they are internal, it is easy to check how they are regarded in the ranks below.

The Nine Types

Three characteristics stand out for me in modern leadership: purpose, authenticity and delivery. In other words: does this chief executive stand for something credible, can you believe them, and will they achieve what they set out to? Each leadership type in this book has some of these characteristics in some form. Some have more than others. The best leaders exhibit all three.

Only once they are appointed can they apply themselves to this three-pronged mission. How they do that helps to define their leadership type. This book tries to understand how each operates, the decisions they take, their motivations and fears.

Leadership success can be hard to judge. Some failures are greatly magnified. Many go by without comment. And a legacy is not worth studying until a few years have passed.

What is clear is that the average corporate challenge is getting bigger and more complex, with larger enterprises, more stakeholders and a greater array of performance targets – including environmental and social – to meet. The leaders that can get the best from their people, challenge their competitors effectively and take calculated risks are a valuable commodity.

Three further points:

Of course, there are some overlaps between my Nine Types. Identifying a pure Lover, Founder or Diplomat is like uncovering a pure bloodline – something of a rarity. But the examples given demonstrate the core attributes of each.

Secondly, leaders can change. In fact, if they don't, they risk foreshortening their careers. But I don't think their leadership type alters so much over the years. A Founder will always be a Founder – who is more likely to sell their company and start again rather than stay on and work for the acquirer – just as a Scion and a Seller are bound respectively by their birth and training.

Finally, leaders do not like to be pigeonholed, unless for the purposes of this book they have been put down as a Campaigner or a Human, two of the most aspirational types. Not everyone will welcome or agree with their classification.

Endnotes

1   Ashton, J (2016) Ericsson's Hans Vestberg: The clean-cut Swede with a need for mobile speed, *The Telegraph*, 3 April. https://www.telegraph.co.uk/business/2016/04/03/ericssons-hans-vestberg-the-clean-cut-swede-with-a-need-for-mobi/ (archived at https://perma.cc/AW37-C2KZ)

2   Smith, C (2016) Getting a job at Goldman Sachs, *efinancialcareers*, 5 May. https://news.efinancialcareers.com/uk-en/243963/getting-a-job-at-goldman-sachs (archived at https://perma.cc/39YC-224A)

3 Day One Team (2019) What is a 'bar raiser' at Amazon?, *aboutamazon*, 9 October. https://blog.aboutamazon.eu/working-at-amazon/what-is-a-bar-raiser-at-amazon (archived at https://perma.cc/69C4-SEFF)

4 Leadership Principles, *Amazon Jobs* https://www.amazon.jobs/en/principles (archived at https://perma.cc/X7F8-4XWK)

5 Haas Edersheim, E (2004) *McKinsey's Marvin Bower: Vision, leadership and the creation of management consulting,* Wiley, Hoboken, New Jersey

6 Ashton, J (2019) Leading with James Ashton Episode 1 – Deloitte and Teenage Cancer Trust [podcast] *Apple Podcasts*, 29 April. https://podcasts.apple.com/gb/podcast/episode-1-deloitte-and-teenage-cancer-trust/id1460796936?i=1000436797958 (archived at https://perma.cc/2B3L-GAFG)

7 Ashton, J (2020) Leading with James Ashton S3 Episode 3 – Bupa [podcast] *Apple Podcasts*, 4 May. https://podcasts.apple.com/gb/podcast/s3-episode-3-bupa/id1460796936?i=1000473511225 (archived at https://perma.cc/CRM8-ZHFJ)

CHAPTER ONE

Alphas

Empire builders

As the curtain rose to reveal a blood-red stage, an expectant hush spread across the 2,000-strong audience settling into their seats in Salzburg's Grosses Festspielhaus. The Austrians take their opera seriously and the performance on this sticky August Saturday night in 2015 promised to be extra special.

About to commence was the highlight of that year's six-week Salzburg Festival: a new interpretation of *Il Trovatore* – The Troubadour – Verdi's masterpiece with choruses so epic that ardent operagoers forgive the over-complicated plot of witchcraft and vengeance.

Crowds had thronged outside Grosses Festspielhaus beforehand, eager to catch a glimpse of dignitaries promenading down the avenue in their black-tie finery to the venue that had been built more than 50 years earlier on the site of the former court stables of the Prince Archbishops of Salzburg. With barely a moment to cool off, the guests processed up the stairs and into the auditorium to admire the 100m-wide stage, one of the largest in the world. There, sat in excellent stalls seats with a large retinue around him, was Peter Brabeck-Letmathe, the beaming chairman of Nestlé, the world's largest food company.

He had visited Salzburg many times before. The city lies a two-hour drive north of his home town of Villach. This event had also become something of a gathering point for the top brass of the company whose brands included KitKat chocolate bars, Cheerios breakfast cereal, Perrier mineral water and Stouffer's frozen food. Nestlé began its sponsorship of the festival in 1991 and from 2010 onwards it has given an award for the best young conductor. The contest gives pause for breath for executives because it falls conveniently just after half-year results are posted, usually at the end of July.

Brabeck-Letmathe, a towering figure in the company with piercing blue eyes and an earnest mien, made no secret of the fact that the Salzburg Festival was one of the highlights of his year. Several of his lieutenants were therefore encouraged to fly in and linger for a day or so. Customers and the media were invited along too, to sample some culture and hear about Nestlé's latest achievements at lunches and dinners that always ended with glossy Nespresso coffee menus being passed around. Brabeck-Letmathe was a keen piano player of modest ability – he said – playing 'only when I am alone'. But that night, as the Vienna Philharmonic struck up a gorgeous melody, it was clear that he was the conductor of his own orchestra.

Alpha leaders are easy to spot. It takes a big character to lead a big, multinational company – at least according to decades of business theory. They are talismen (which should of course be talismans) – rarely women – who expect to be the most important person in any room they walk into. They are inspiring to follow, a little scary even. Their workforce hang on their every word and members of their court fret at how new developments will be received by them. They are tough and top-down traditional, doing things the way they have always been done, a fixed point around which strategy and direction can gather. No other leadership type could have muscled its way into this book's first chapter.

Alphas exert power over an organization from their force of personality channelled down clear lines of command. Many deny it happens, but how Alphas operate belies the idea that leadership is somehow a group activity. These extensive responsibilities are not taken lightly. Blessed with fierce self-belief, Alphas are immaculately turned out and drive themselves as hard as the organizations they lead. They also amass baubles of power: the biggest office or the shiniest yacht.

Corporate scale and longevity are two measures of Alpha status and Brabeck-Letmathe had both in spades. By the time he took his seat for the concert that evening he had spent 47 years at the company, on his way to completing five decades of service. Nestlé feeds and waters the world and counted 339,000 staff and annual sales of £60 billion on his watch. Such reach afforded great power and drew him into the worlds of politics, agriculture and wider society, battling with shareholders, rival food companies and policymakers to run his company the way he saw fit.

Brabeck-Letmathe was not afraid to embrace controversy. Nestlé was scarred for many years by the scandal over breast milk substitute (BMS). The issue can be traced back to 1977 when the Nestlé boycott was launched in the United States by INFACT (Infant Formula Action Coalition) to protest against unethical marketing. The company was accused of inhibiting the development of millions of babies in the developing world by aggressively targeting new mothers with formula milk when breast milk was a healthier and cheaper option.

More recently, the chairman stirred debate by insisting that access to water was not a human right. That was quite something from the head of the firm that sells millions of bottles of Nestlé Pure Life and Buxton every year, but his point was that water is a human right for the 25 to 50 litres needed per day for hydration and minimum hygiene. That makes up 1.5 per cent of the water that is being withdrawn from the system. Everything else, from filling swimming pools and watering golf courses, should not be covered by that right.

Scaling the heights

The scale and breadth of Nestlé lent Brabeck-Letmathe the power to engage with world leaders and others at the highest level. But it was not the only reason he was keen to defend it. 'I think at the back of everybody's mind we always have this idea that small is beautiful and big is a little bit ugly,'[1] he said when talking about how consumers were turning their backs on mass-produced groceries in favour of small-batch, organic, locally sourced and gluten-free options. Brabeck-Letmathe argued that too much focus would damage Nestlé's long-term growth because it tended to starve investment in new markets and products. Slow-growing divisions such as dried pasta could be hived off but to grow at the rate that shareholders were demanding meant it was better to have a broad portfolio, he believed.

The numbers tended to bear that theory out. Until 2008, after serving as chief executive for 11 years, Brabeck-Letmathe delivered top-line growth of at least 5 per cent and improving profit margins. Nestlé was replete with long-term projects that had been anything but an overnight success. They included the Nespresso coffee capsule system, popularized by an advertising campaign starring George Clooney, but which took 25 years to properly develop.

Brabeck-Letmathe also championed a drive beyond food into nutrition and healthcare with Nestlé Health Science, which was trying to discover treatments for gastrointestinal conditions and to combat the effects of chemotherapy. Another venture, Nestlé Skin Health, a developer of creams and acne treatments, was the product of a 30-year joint venture with beauty firm L'Oréal. Here was a strong and steady company, able to place long-term bets and see them through to fruition.

The choreography of Brabeck-Letmathe's leadership was interesting. When he stood aside as chief executive in 2008 – hanging on to the role of chairman – he claimed to have done so early so that his close colleague Paul Bulcke could have a longer run at the role. The pair had worked together in Latin America earlier in their careers and knew each other so well they spoke Spanish to each other even though one was Belgian, the other Austrian.

But in standing down, Brabeck-Letmathe actually preserved his own power base, remaining chairman for almost a decade until 2017. He is still chairman emeritus. 'I have always said a chief executive is successful when his successor is as successful as he was,'[2] he said.

In the ensuing years, life has become harder for all packaged goods companies but Nestlé has continued to outperform. In 2017 Mark Schneider became the first outsider chief executive appointed to lead the company in almost a century. He sped up new product innovation and traded assets, most notably striking a £5.2 billion deal with Starbucks in 2018 to develop its coffee range that is sold in supermarkets around the world. The group's breadth gave him options when drawing up his strategy that has involved tightening the portfolio around faster-growing sectors. The skin health division, including brands Cetaphil and Proactiv, which might not have been nurtured without an Alpha's touch, became a useful asset to offload in 2019 for $10 billion.

Attaining Alpha status is as much to do with how a leader's presence is felt across a company as it is with standing in a room. Brabeck-Letmathe's personal strength is worth noting. In his later years as chairman, he was treated for a 'curable illness' that caused him to lose his hair. Rather than slowing down, he appeared to speed up. His doctor banned him from flying long distances, a tough demand for any jet-setting Alpha to accede to. But Brabeck-Letmathe put the spare time to excellent use, qualifying as a helicopter pilot. Everyone in Nestlé knew he was not to be messed with – and not to be stopped in the way that mere mortals might be by age or medical complaint.

This personal strength is a constant theme among this type of leader. You would think an Alpha had enough on his or her plate running their company but there is quite often evidence that they feel they must excel in their private life too. That competitive streak extends to compiling an impressive hinterland – as this next leader demonstrates.

António Horta-Osório took on one of the biggest challenges in Corporate Britain in 2011 when he attempted to revive Lloyds Banking Group after the financial crisis and lead it out of state ownership. The Black Horse bank was once one of the largest in the world but latterly concentrated on building a rock-solid domestic franchise. Lloyds was brought low after agreeing to a government-brokered rescue of ailing lender HBOS in 2008 that meant it was forced to accept its own £20 billion rescue by the taxpayer soon after.

This was more than just a banking job. When it was working properly, Lloyds supported whole swathes of the economy. When it wasn't, small businesses and mortgage customers stood to suffer. On appointment in November 2010, Horta-Osório made clear he understood 'the vitally important role the Group plays in the UK's social and economic fabric'.[3]

There is much you should understand about the Portuguese Horta-Osório, and that insight starts a long way from the boardroom. His love of tennis comes from his father, who was a table tennis champion. Doctors told the young banker he would never play again after breaking his right wrist at the age of 30. He promptly taught himself to play left-handed, reverting to right-handed two years later. Talk about gritty. And he speaks six languages. At risk of veering off into caricature, he is known to enjoy scuba diving with sharks. Oh,

THE NINE TYPES OF LEADER

and his favourite book is *The Art of War*, by Sun Tzu, the ancient Chinese military text that became a leadership must-read, offering lessons about discipline and humility.

This personal determination extends to his business life. Horta-Osório was poached by Lloyds from the Spanish bank Santander's UK offshoot, where the challenge that faced him was of a different order. He was driving himself so hard when he took over that within the first year he was diagnosed with sleep deprivation and given several weeks off – an extremely rare incident among blue-chip bosses who typically battle with relentless pressure but don't buckle under it.

What marks out Horta-Osório is that from this early wobble he came back even stronger. Later on, he made a convincing defence for strong, solo leadership – the Alpha method in a nutshell – regardless of the obvious strain it can breed. Those intense turnarounds, he said, required 'a more centralized approach to management because you are under pressure. Like we used to say in Portugal, in times of war, you don't clean weapons.'4

Horta-Osório might have been a Fixer (see Chapter 2) if it wasn't for the fact he has endured for so long at the helm of Lloyds, disclosing plans in mid-2020 that he intended to stand down in 2021. With 65,000 staff, 30 million customers, the biggest private shareholder base in the country and originator of one in four mortgages for first-time buyers, there are a lot of people relying on him to get it right. It is a challenge he clearly relishes. He even looks like an Alpha leader, straight from central casting: tanned and strong, with slicked-back leonine hair, sharp suit, and a handshake almost as firm as his eye contact. It is clear who is in charge when he joins a meeting.

His skill has been in grinding out results. Lloyds returned to the dividend list in 2015 and the UK government sold its final stake in the bank in 2017. It was an easier fix than Royal Bank of Scotland, its fellow state-backed lender, but that is not to underplay Horta-Osório's achievements. He also understood early on that making Lloyds perform better was not just about sorting out the financials. It had to be a good corporate citizen too. In getting his arms around such a large business he has earned authenticity – something that Alphas often struggle with. It is a fundamental trait of Lovers, a leadership type of which more in Chapter 6.

For one interview, Lloyds' public relations handlers were determined that their boss would be photographed quickly in one of the many bland, beige rooms the bank keeps for meetings on its executive floor. Persuaded of the importance of the image, Horta-Osório reluctantly agreed to go onto the balcony where the snapper had set up his equipment – just as long as it was not wet. 'You English call this "not raining?"' he said, stepping out into the lightest of drizzles. Horta-Osório posed, briefly, against the glorious backdrop of the Square Mile's skyline and an angry, gun-metal grey sky. Truly an Alpha setting.

A company is a collection of tangible, fixed assets, such as factories and warehouses, and intangibles: brands, intellectual property, even a culture that takes root. Alphas can shape all of this in their own image if they are effective enough. Whether they should is another matter.

Dame Marjorie Scardino's reign at Pearson is a good example. Sometimes an Alpha is required if a company is to be reinvented over a long period. Sometimes shareholders are willingly led if they are convinced the prize is large enough – and the person at the top has instilled them with great faith in the future.

Dame Marjorie inherited a jumbled conglomerate when she became chief executive of Pearson in 1997 – the first female leader of a FTSE 100 company. What was originally a Yorkshire engineering firm had diversified over decades so that its assets included stakes in satellite giant BSkyB, investment bank Lazard, waxwork attraction Madame Tussauds and even an avocado farm.

There was a stack of consulting projects awaiting the next chief executive, each exploring a new angle on what to do next. Here the notion of a broad portfolio that Brabeck-Letmathe had championed at Nestlé had few fans. At least a range of grocery lines shares customers and distribution channels. Pearson was in no way integrated.

From the consultants' reports and her own investigations, Dame Marjorie concluded that education – textbooks, teaching materials and classroom testing – was the future, even though it constituted an extremely small part of the group at that time. Anyone who knew her might have guessed that that would be the direction she pursued. Her career was studded with knowledge and information sharing, from founding the campaigning *Georgia Gazette* newspaper with her husband Albert in her native United States to leading *The Economist* newspaper for five years from 1992. Now education was calling, with the promise that the internet could personalize lifelong learning for all.

Dame Marjorie's style was folksy but firm. The former rodeo rider became known for her dry wit and down-to-earth 'Dear Everyone' staff emails – an openness not typical of Alphas. She tried to insist that steering the company down a new path was a group effort but that did not wash. 'Pearson is made up of a lot of people. I get to talk more than they do, but they have their say,' she said.[5]

Dame Marjorie surrounded herself with people who bought into her plan and steadfastly set the parameters for success, backed by Lord Stevenson, the group's chairman and a key supporter. Pearson had plenty of assets to sell off so that funds could be recycled into education. But in 2002 she made clear the group's crown jewel, the *Financial Times*, would be sold 'over my dead body'. Most chief executives can rarely be so plain – but Alphas can.

This boldness and remarkable air cover provided by Stevenson imbued Pearson with a sense of mission over and above the aim of merely delivering improving returns. In pursuit of those, investors were unusually patient because this transformation involved a steep learning curve.

In 2000, Pearson's expensive, high-tech acquisition of National Computer Systems was poorly communicated to the City. Dame Marjorie's comments at the time of the deal read like a speech from a campaign rally. 'Together, we can create the "intelligent classroom", where teaching is customized so that each child learns in his own way, at his own speed, with constant assessment, feedback and help,' she said. 'Together we can take the next great leap in education – adding applications and testing to curriculum and changing the way we teach and learn.'[6] There was no room for dissent.

Meanwhile, a bold ambition to double the share price in five years became an albatross around the stock's neck. Pearson achieved that feat very quickly during the dotcom bubble but it proved to be unsustainable and the shares actually went backwards over the prescribed timeframe. But across Dame Marjorie's entire 15-year reign, Pearson's sales tripled to nearly £6 billion, as did profits, which reached a then-record £942 million in 2011, the last year before she departed.

Two years later, in summer 2015, the *FT* was finally sold for £844 million to Japanese media group Nikkei. As she retired, Dame Marjorie left the door open to the transaction she famously ruled out, although of course she would no longer be in charge to stop it happening. 'People are mistaken to think that we are religious about anything,' she said. 'They have always been mistaken about me; they never understood that.'[7]

From 2013 the company was led by John Fallon, Pearson's former communications director and one of Dame Marjorie's first hires. He fared less well than his mentor as textbook sales stalled and free alternatives to paid-for teaching tools were developed by digital rivals. Keeping an Alpha at the helm would doubtless have been more effective in keeping investors at bay – but only as long as the company eventually delivered on what its visionary leader promised.

Rise and fall

It is worth mentioning how quickly business empires can fail when the renowned Alphas that masterminded their creation have departed. The industrialist Lord (Arnold) Weinstock spent 33 years until 1996 leading GEC, one of Britain's great conglomerates. Weinstock took the helm of his father-in-law's electronics firm, increased turnover

110-fold and created a steady business that straddled electronics, defence and shipbuilding and featured famous industrial names such as Hotpoint and Avery. Soon after his retirement in 1996, the company – renamed Marconi – was unpicked by managers who drove it disastrously into internet equipment just as the spending bubble burst, burning through a carefully conserved cash pile. It was taken over by its creditors in 2003.

Alphas become associated with empire building, which is equated to indulgent leadership that breeds inefficiency. The contrary view is that a spread of assets and geographies can bring with it stability. Either way, Alphas offer strong management – even if that means holding together corporations and warring leadership teams through a sheer force. They are resolutely committed, if a little domineering. It can be preferable to what comes afterwards.

The long view

Not dissimilar to Lord Weinstock, Stefano Pessina has made his company his life's work. He has transformed his family's small Italian drugs distributor into Walgreens Boots Alliance (WBA), one of the largest drugs retail groups in the world with a $50 billion stock market value in good times. Like all the best Alphas, he has taken his time to get here. It took five years of persuasion to engineer a merger of his distribution business Alliance UniChem with the UK's struggling high street stalwart Boots in 2005. That combined business was taken private in 2007 backed by the financial might of private equity group KKR.

Throughout it all the Italian was a nerveless visionary, seeing potential in Boots' shops – as community hubs underpinned by a steady stream of income from National Health Service prescriptions – that few institutional investors could see. He also kept calm as the company was loaded with debt just as the credit crunch threatened to topple over-borrowed companies.

Leading up to this point, Pessina had been on the acquisition trail through Italy and France, snapping up small distributors and encountering the pharmacist and businesswoman Ornella Barra. She would go on to become WBA's co-chief operating officer and his partner in business and life – underscoring the Alpha tenet that the personal and the professional are entwined.

Even before the ink was dry on the Boots deal, Pessina was a step ahead, having begun work on finding a US partner that in 2012 turned out to be Walgreens, a retailer that in the United States was every bit as well known as Boots in the UK. And before the two-stage transaction with Walgreens was completed, his head was turned by opportunities in China that in 2017 crystallized in an investment in one of the country's largest national pharmacy chains, Sinopharm Holding GuoDa Drugstores (GuoDa). Some 1,900 stores from Rite Aid, the US drugstore chain, were also added in 2018.

'I have always believed that particularly the wholesale business needed global players because the manufacturers, our suppliers, are global,' he said in 2014. 'I was surprised that the market didn't have any.'[8]

Bespectacled, with a mane of white hair, Pessina's professorial appearance places him tinkering at a laboratory bench in a white coat or making up prescriptions in the back of a corner store. But this unconventional boardroom tycoon – who talks slowly in careful English, often with his arms folded and eyes closed – has been relentless in turning his vision into reality, creating an empire operating in 25 countries with 370 drug distribution depots and more than 3,000 health and beauty shops. Still, he divides opinion, portrayed as either a corporate alchemist who rescued an ailing Boots, or the worst form of barbarian at the gate.

What few can deny is his ability to endure. When Pessina was expected to stand down as Alliance Boots and Walgreens finally united in 2014, it was actually the younger man, Walgreens chief executive Greg Wasson, who announced he was leaving. Pessina's ballast is his ownership. With a 16 per cent shareholding in WBA, he remains the largest investor in the enlarged group. But he also has a grip on long-term strategy, although the non-retailer's belief in the power of bricks and mortar has been severely tested during and after the 2020 Covid-19 outbreak. Rumours have swirled that WBA may be taken private in another record-breaking buy-out so it can be restructured away from the scrutiny of quarterly reporting. Public or private, you can be sure that Pessina will continue to hold sway, like many long-lasting Alphas, with Barra by his side.

Wounded beasts

The morning after the opening ceremony of the London Olympics in July 2012, Jeff Immelt was holed up in a marketing suite next to St Pancras railway station. Outside, digital characters strode across a giant LED display that was wrapped around the building, in front of which children played in the sunshine. Inside, the boss of one of the world's largest manufacturing companies was feeling far less active. Although he ran one of the International Olympic Committee's 11 top-tier sponsors, Immelt was forced to watch the antics of Bond, Bean and Beckham and the parachuting Queen Elizabeth II on television. Three broken ribs had made it too painful to travel to the stadium at the revitalized Stratford in East London. The next day he was still shuffling painfully on the sofa.

Here was an Alpha displaying unfamiliar frailty. No hard-driving captain of industry relishes a reminder that they are merely human. All the worse if such weakness is on display to the outside world. But the blow barely made Immelt less high-powered than usual, as he raced through a series of meetings that had been sliced into 15-minute portions to fit his breakneck schedule. With a gleaming, all-American grin and vice-like handshake, Immelt was also impressively high wattage – as befits the leader of the home of Thomas Edison's lightbulbs, an innovation that had transformed home life for millions of Americans more than a century earlier. And if anyone was unclear of his status, dangling around his neck was his laminated Olympics accreditation with the word 'TOP' printed in bold letters.

Beyond lightbulbs, General Electric had gone on to sell far bigger pieces of infrastructure: power generators, medical scanners, wind turbines, aircraft engines, locomotives and oil and gas kit. Employing 300,000 staff, it had established itself as one of the United States' industrial bellwethers with an impressive international reach. The chief executive since

2001, Immelt succeeded the legendary Alpha boss Jack Welch, whose 'rank and yank' policy reputedly offloaded 10 per cent of the company's weakest performers every year. Immelt's recipe for keeping on top of it all was simple: 'You have got to have a big desire, a big motor and you've got to have a certain sense for yourself – be self-reflective.'[9]

By 2012 GE appeared as powerful as ever, but looking back it was just as patched up as its boss. In 2009 and 2010, the company had been forced to cut its previously untouchable dividend as the financial crisis bit. Immelt was busy trying to reshape GE, offloading chemicals and insurance businesses, as well as NBC, the US TV network, and shrinking GE Capital, the group's finance arm which had been the source of much of its troubles. Yet his international vision of supplying more goods to more territories was found wanting. Just as the US economy began to take off, the rebuilt dividend was cut again in 2017 and 2018, by which point Immelt had gone. The conglomerate that once could do no wrong was found to be flabby and unfocused and in need of further slimming down by his successors.

Out of fashion

The last decade has shown that business empires are out of fashion – and so are empire builders that seek to sit on top of them. Alphas are less in demand than just about any other type of leader.

Shareholders question the merits of scale; society isn't so sure about globalization. Power should not be absolute – it should have the requisite checks and balances.

The leaders who champion bigger is better have to tread a careful path and find headspace for such things as account-ability and inclusivity. Sharpening performance, under-standing the consumer and embracing the interests of all stakeholders are tasks that Fixers, Sellers and Diplomats are better placed to get right. Their attributes will be explored in later chapters. It has been a rude awakening for some Alphas who think they can do everything themselves. When these world beaters take a beating, it can get messy.

Sir Philip Green was the self-styled King of the High Street, with 3,000 shops across five continents. Since acquir-ing the Arcadia group in 2002, the tycoon had a unique reach in the fashion world with brands including Topshop, Topman, Dorothy Perkins and Miss Selfridge. He used that clout to devastating effect, threatening to pull his advertis-ing from newspapers that did not reflect his success generously.

Tanned, with grey, slicked-back curls, sporting his cus-tomary uniform of dark suit and white, open-necked shirt, Sir Philip was typically combative and confident. He had no problem reminding guests to his boardroom, high above the shopping mecca of London's Oxford Street, how busy he was yet how closely he remained to the minutiae of his business. That omnipotence, real or imagined, is typical Alpha behaviour. In one interview that took place in 2013 as he prepared for international expansion with dozens of franchise openings in the pipeline – many of them within the US group Nordstrom's department stores – he passed his battered old Nokia phone across the table to share a text message exchange. Timed at 4.15 am, one missive read:

'Mary wants to know why you're not asleep?' The quick reply was: 'Because I'm keeping an eye on all of you lot.'[10]

Sir Philip's grasp sought to extend beyond his own business to everyone else's in the sector, opining on trading conditions, store fascia, staff training and tax policy. He ensured that the Topshop catwalk show became a staple of London Fashion Week, with model Kate Moss and fashion's grande dame, Anna Wintour, frequent guests on the front row. Not bad for someone who learned his trade selling shoes to shops from the age of 16. This Alpha was a trader, progressing to the peak of the industry by buying and selling a string of retailers, including Jean Jeanie and Sears, suffering a rare setback only when he stood down from Amber Day in 1992 when investors demanded his head after profits fell short.

Sir Philip's fortunes peaked in 2005, when he drew a bumper £1.2 billion dividend from Arcadia, four times the group's pre-tax profit that year. It was paid to his wife Lady Tina, the group's owner and a Monaco resident.

Matters looked far bleaker a decade later. His department store chain BHS was sold for £1 to Dominic Chappell, a serial bankrupt, only for it to collapse after a year with the loss of 11,000 jobs. Critics wondered how a details man could have let that happen. Amid a storm of protest, and calls for him to be stripped of his knighthood, Sir Philip contributed £363 million to the BHS pension scheme.

Arcadia has also struggled, undone by fast-fashion rivals H&M, Zara and Primark and nimble online competitors ASOS and Boohoo. In 2019, creditors approved a series of rent cuts and store closures but there was very likely more downsizing to come. Pressure on the group was compounded by the Covid-19 pandemic's devastating impact on the High Street. Sir Philip has been shown up for fighting the wrong battles by failing to meet the digital challenge.

One growth market remains the media. Sir Philip's reign – or something very like it – has been chronicled in books and a movie, *Greed*, starring comedian Steve Coogan in the lead role. Marketed with the strapline 'The devil's in the retail', it was no hagiography.

Banking on a big name

Alphas do not have to be long-serving company men or self-made entrepreneurs. They can emerge at the top of public institutions too. Skipping from the high street to high finance might seem a leap too far but what the next Alpha has in common with the last is power through personality.

When Chancellor George Osborne began hunting for the next Governor of the Bank of England in 2012 he was keen to find a figure that befitted London's standing as a global financial hub. In Mark Carney he was not disappointed. The Governor of the Bank of Canada had already made waves on the world stage, having emerged from the financial crisis relatively unscathed and sporting an easy charm and movie-star good looks rarely found among the ranks of dry central bankers. He was the first non-national to take the helm of the Threadneedle Street institution, but having studied at Oxford and further schooled by serving

13 years at the investment bank Goldman Sachs he was deemed ideal for the post. Osborne was so keen to get his man that he allowed Carney to sign up for a five-year term when the advertised tenure was eight – although the turbulence caused by Brexit meant in the event he served almost seven years.

Carney was like no Governor the Bank had ever had before. The 326-year-old institution was of critical importance but had never really needed a big personality to lead it. The Bank's Alpha presence across the Square Mile was not dependent on Alpha leadership. In fact, it bred a model of understatement. Back in time, just an eyebrow raised at the right moment during fireside chats with whichever chief executive had been called in for a discreet word was deemed sufficient for the smooth running of the City's regulatory force.

However, Carney's appointment fed the notion that the City of London had the pull to attract big figures from across the globe. At the Lord Mayor's Mansion House banquet for bankers in June 2004, Lord King, Carney's predecessor, talked about the 'Wimbledonisation' of the City, which was, as he put it, 'hosting a successful tournament where most of the winners come from overseas'.[11]

On the one hand, Carney was visibly high-powered on the international stage, combining his domestic duties with chairmanship of the Financial Stability Board (FSB), an international body that monitors and makes recommendations about the global financial system. On the other hand, he was verging on cool and youthful, spotted relaxing in lilac polo shirt and shorts at the upmarket Wilderness Festival in leafy Oxfordshire and often sporting a grey-and-black Swatch

watch instead of a chunky Rolex, which is standard issue for most banking titans.

But this Alpha had a job to do unlike any of his predecessors. Carney needed to shore up faith in the system of financial regulation that had been sorely tested during the financial crisis. In order to do that, a few months before he arrived an extra 1,300 staff were added to the organization from the defunct Financial Services Authority watchdog. It meant the Bank combined financial stability with its broad remit that already featured monetary policy – including the setting of interest rates – and regulation of the banking system. Like Dame Marjorie Scardino at Pearson, Carney argued unconvincingly that running the Bank was a joint effort. 'It is not about me, we run the institution as the governors,'[12] he said, referring at the time to his four deputies and the Bank's chief operating officer.

Here was an Alpha who led from the front, and didn't at all mind the spotlight. But his vaunting ambition was hard to live up to and Carney showed he was human after all. Two prongs of his strategy were notable. Criticized for its opacity in the past, Carney set out to ensure the Bank gave clarity to markets about the direction of travel for interest rates. Unfortunately his flagship policy of forward guidance, which pegged an interest rate rise to the trigger of falling unemployment, was quickly dropped as the jobless total shrank without the expected improvement in the economy.

Interest rates moved only a handful of times on his watch. These were tumultuous years, with the Brexit vote of 2016 and heightened geopolitical tensions. But far from telegraphing the mood, traders and investors were left guessing right to the end of his reign in March 2020 about which way rates would go next.

Carney also set about improving the transparency, diversity and general smooth running of the Bank, which was suspected to suffer from a culture of deference and groupthink. That was dealt a blow in 2017, when one of his newly appointed deputies, the well-connected Charlotte Hogg, resigned after a row over failing to report conflicts of interest. The Bank also struggled to stay on track towards meeting its diversity targets, particularly in senior BAME representation. Carney wrote to the chair of the Treasury Select Committee in 2019 to admit: 'There is scope for further improvements and we are continuing to look for ways to maintain momentum on Diversity and Inclusion.'[13]

He took criticism badly but where the diminutive Carney excelled was on the big stage, especially his deft actions to calm financial markets in the days after the surprise Brexit referendum result in June 2016. His appointment was an experiment and not a wholly successful one. Hence Carney's successor from March 2020 could not be more different: a far-from-Alpha figure, the long-serving Bank veteran Andrew Bailey.

Technology titans

Sitting atop a spaghetti of subway lines, the Fulton Center is a gateway to Lower Manhattan, disgorging thousands of workers into New York's financial district every day. And sitting at the top of this futuristic mall and transport hub with its web of escalators and stairways is what occupied many millions of square feet all over the city: WeWork.

Since it first opened its doors in 2010, the co-working start-up colonized urban areas all over the world and became the largest office tenant in New York and London. Its developments were feted by property developers and mayors alike, eager to bring some excitement to their investments and down-at-heel districts with the prospect of buzzy young entrepreneurs moving in.

Sure enough, in this doughnut ring of space in the Fulton Center there was a well-stocked bar, exposed brickwork, low-slung sofas, some curious graffiti and hipsters draped artfully around the place gazing at laptops and smartphones. At the centre of it all sat Adam Neumann, eager to explain why his workers somehow existed on a higher plane compared with those scuttling commuters far below.

Neumann was an Alpha cut from a different cloth. Not for him the expensive tailoring that corporate titans of the past sported. Handsome and clear-eyed, his office outfit was a black hoodie and beanie hat from which his dark, glossy locks spilled out. But his casual appearance made him no less powerful.

In many industries, the overweening figurehead has been dying out in favour of something more collegiate and transparent. In the main, the next generation of leaders looks very different from the last. But in the technology space, Alphas have been rebooted.

There is no other way to describe this crop of young leaders. They preach a shared, liberal future but in fact have amassed more control over their staff, company and even society at large than Alphas from years gone by could ever have imagined.

Neumann turned shared office space into a near-religious experience. 'I want to teach people that creating your life's work is the secret – not trying to make a living,'[14] he said, likening the group's pace of expansion to the growth of the Roman Empire. Whether religion or army, by early 2017 WeWork had amassed plenty of followers: nearly 130,000 members in 45 cities on five continents.

Neumann favoured social glue to keep them aligned. His staff dined together at the start of the week, part of a Thank God It's Monday initiative, and then worked through, sometimes as late as 3 am. Tequila swigging was encouraged. In interviews, his zeal could not be contained to new openings and one day achieving profitability. Neumann wanted to discuss vision. WeWork was not an office company, he pointed out. Its secret was its operating system that could design and manage the layout of commercial and residential buildings anywhere in the world with a few touches of a button. He was a messianic town planner, enlivened by the prospect of designing new, environmentally friendly cities from scratch. 'We want to build things like stadiums and amphitheatres where people come together,'[15] he said. Ideas for schools, apartments and even an airline followed. Neumann had lofty Alpha aspirations, not goals, and bestrode a corporate structure that offered no clue how to get there.

What powered his ambition was many billions of pounds of backing from SoftBank, the Japanese investor whose Vision Fund placed giant bets on emerging technologies. SoftBank is not alone. Across the landscape of new technologies, investors are backing Alphas who are visionaries in the hope of tapping sources of explosive growth. These are many of the same shareholders that do not mourn the passing of Alphas at General Electric and other traditional corporations, who were replaced by leaders encouraged to focus their sprawling conglomerates, slash costs, drive shareholder value and pursue a sustainable agenda. Yet in the technology world the next generation of Alphas – many of whom are Founders too – has discovered an avenue in which to prosper. For a broad, disconnected portfolio, read the moonshot division of Google; for the dominating personality, think of Jack Dorsey at Twitter who was allowed to do pretty much as he pleased, despite poor shareholder returns, until the activist investor Elliott Management began calling for his dismissal.

So much private money has been chasing the best ideas that these firms have been able to come to the stock market later than they might otherwise have done. Their principals have kept far greater control of the venture for longer. It means that today's Alphas are the technology titans who will not be told how to behave, such as Mark Zuckerberg at Facebook, Amazon's Jeff Bezos or Tesla's Elon Musk. When Snap, the company behind social media service Snapchat, listed its shares in New York in March 2018 it did so with no voting rights attached at all so founders Evan Spiegel and Bobby Murphy could retain control of the board.

Ceding so much to these new-wave Alphas has frequently paid off for shareholders. Soaring share prices and exceptional performance delivered by the likes of the late Steve Jobs at Apple have made Wall Street their supplicants. But every so often, culture tramples over vision, such as the necessary ousting of Travis Kalanick from the helm of ride-sharing app Uber. The particular strengths and weaknesses of Founders are explored in another chapter.

Ultimately WeWork didn't work in the way its leaders had hoped. A stock market flotation planned for September 2019 was canned after a vague company prospectus rattled investors and revealed unacceptable conflicts, such as Neumann's leasing back to WeWork – now called the We Company – properties that he part-owned. The firm's valuation was slashed from $47 billion to $5 billion and thousands of jobs were lost. The charismatic Neumann departed. An agreement for Softbank to acquire his shares in the company for a reported $1 billion collapsed, resulting in legal action.

Alphas do not completely belong in a bygone era, although they are an endangered species. What has not changed for them is that power is bestowed by persuasion and performance. Those capable of delivering great, uncompromising leadership can continue to thrive. Yet even the most committed, inspirational and fearsome must submit themselves to greater scrutiny, checks and balances. And those Alphas whose promises do not pay off will find themselves replaced by another leadership type.

ALPHAS IN BRIEF

Strengths: Visionary, energetic, inspiring, tough, traditional.

Weaknesses: Inflexible, narrow-minded, failure to listen, failure to adapt.

Suitability: Leading big, multinational companies with many moving parts, large workforces, disparate locations and regulatory challenges.

Where you will find them: In fewer boardrooms than you used to as a consensual leadership style is favoured.

Endnotes

1   Ashton J (2015) Peter Brabeck-Letmathe: Nestlé Head sceptical about health benefits of the gluten-free revolution, *Independent*, 10 August. https://www.independent.co.uk/news/uk/home-news/peter-brabeck-letmathe-nestle-head-sceptical-about-health-benefits-of-the-gluten-free-revolution-10447571.html (archived at https://perma.cc/7ZQJ-5EB3)

2   Ashton J (2014) Nestlé chairman Peter Brabeck-Letmathe: 'I plan to leave my food empire in good health', *Evening Standard*, 9 May. https://www.standard.co.uk/business/markets/nestl-chairman-peter-brabeck-letmathe-i-plan-to-leave-my-food-empire-in-good-health-9343265.html (archived at https://perma.cc/7KKY-48L2)

3   Lloyds Banking Group (2010) Appointment of new Chief Executive Officer. https://www.lloydsbankinggroup.com/globalassets/documents/investors/2010/2010nov3_lbg_new_ceo.pdf (archived at https://perma.cc/CJ9K-PEZZ)

4   Ashton, J (2014) The City's top feminist? Lloyds CEO António Horta-Osório on his plans for the bank, *Evening Standard*, 5 March. https://www.standard.co.uk/lifestyle/london-life/the-city-s-top-feminist-lloyds-ceo-antonio-horta-os-rio-on-his-plans-for-the-bank-9170813.html (archived at https://perma.cc/53MQ-CRVD)

5   Ashton, J (2011) The indispensables: What price the key men of commerce? *The Times*, 23 January. https://www.thetimes.co.uk/article/the-indispensables-what-price-the-key-men-of-commerce-9bn23zpbjq0 (archived at https://perma.cc/MQD9-UBF2)

6   Pearson (2000) Pearson PLC to acquire National Computer Systems, Inc, *Pearson*, 31 July. https://www.pearson.com/en-gb/news-and-research/announcements/2000/07/pearson-plc-to-acquire-national-computer-systems-inc.html#:~:text=Cash%20tender%20offer%20of%20%2473,on%20Friday%2028%20July%2C%202000 (archived at https://perma.cc/E7QL-NK6J)

7   Ashton, J (2012) First Lady of the Footsie prepares to write a new chapter, *Evening Standard*, 5 October. https://www.standard.co.uk/business/markets/first-lady-of-the-footsie-prepares-to-write-a-new-chapter-8199097.html (archived at https://perma.cc/5NWJ-WDX5)

8   Ashton, J (2014) Alliance Boots' Stefano Pessina: Deals are still my
    drug, says the tycoon loath to hang up his Boots, *Evening Standard,* 14
    February. https://www.standard.co.uk/business/markets/alliance-boots-
    stefano-pessina-deals-are-still-my-drug-says-the-tycoon-loath-to-hang-
    up-his-boots-9128017.html (archived at https://perma.cc/6FJ7-YRQ2)

9   Ashton, J (2012) Jeff Immelt: All-American hero powers through the
    downturn, *Independent,* 31 July. https://www.independent.co.uk/news/
    business/analysis-and-features/jeff-immelt-all-american-hero-powers-
    through-the-downturn-7988119.html (archived at https://perma.cc/
    ADK7-M2C6)

10 Ashton, J (2013) London's retail tycoon Sir Philip Green wants the top
    shop from Berlin to Beijing, *Evening Standard,* 4 October. https://www.
    standard.co.uk/business/markets/london-s-retail-tycoon-sir-philip-
    green-wants-the-top-shop-from-berlin-to-beijing-8859149.html
    (archived at https://perma.cc/4XTW-AZCY)

11 King, M (2004) Speech given by Mervyn King, Governor of the Bank
    of England. At the Lord Mayor's Banquet for Bankers and Merchants
    of the City of London at the Mansion House, 16 June. https://www.
    bankofengland.co.uk/-/media/boe/files/speech/2004/mervyn-king-
    mansion-house.pdf (archived at https://perma.cc/4XTW-AZCY)

12 Ashton, J (2014) Mark Carney: the hotdesking Governor of the Bank
    of England who runs to work, *Evening Standard,* 12 December. https://
    www.standard.co.uk/business/business-news/mark-carney-the-
    hotdesking-governor-of-the-bank-of-england-who-runs-to-
    work-9920553.html (archived at https://perma.cc/3J36-GWUT)

13 Carney, M (2019) Letter from the Governor to the Chair of the
    Treasury Committee regarding diversity, *Bank of England,* 19 March.
    https://www.bankofengland.co.uk/-/media/boe/files/letter/2019/
    governor-letter-to-chair-of-tsc-re-diversity-at-the-bank-of-england.pdf?l
    a=en&hash=D588207B004374CDF5E70C787A69922C701098FF
    (archived at https://perma.cc/3YB5-BGB8)

14 Ashton, J (2017) Hipsters, I'm landlord to the gig economy, *The
    Sunday Times,* 26 March. https://www.thetimes.co.uk/article/
    hipsters-im-landlord-to-the-gig-economy-qpdx7qjxj (archived at
    https://perma.cc/WT86-FXLV)

15 Ibid.

CHAPTER TWO

Fixers

Special delivery

Dame Moya Greene calls it her hurry-up moment. Late on a hot, sticky Friday afternoon in August 2010, just as the depleted ranks of London office workers were about to depart for the long Bank Holiday weekend, a chance conversation convinced her that the Royal Mail was in a crisis deeper than even she had first anticipated.

A member of her finance department – not her finance director, she didn't have one then after the previous incumbent quit – casually informed the Canadian that cashflow was so poor the company might not make the next month's payroll. 'Whatever you were thinking and however fast you were going, you better pick the pace up,' Dame Moya recalled telling herself.

She already knew she had a challenge on her hands: that's why she took the job that had begun only six weeks earlier. The Royal Mail – the British institution whose whistling postmen and mistresses and stamps that carry the Queen's head were synonymous with the UK's national identity – was battling to stay alive as letter volumes collapsed, trade unions revolted and its finances stuttered. Dame Moya wanted not only to modernize Royal Mail, which traced its origins back to the time of Henry VIII, but to wrestle it free from state control. Privatization was something that not even the prime minister Margaret Thatcher, the great seller of the nation's assets, had countenanced during the heady 1980s.

Dame Moya is a Fixer, a type of leader drawn to seemingly impossible situations. She described herself as 'highly focused on what needs fixing. If it ain't broke I don't waste time with it. I'm not a caretaker CEO.' Fixers are fire-fighting chiefs, unafraid to step onto a burning platform and seek out a rescue solution. In a relentless corporate world where only the fittest survive, casualties are all too common. Disruption is nothing new but the effects of technology, globalization and regulation appear to be accelerating. A 2017 study by the investment bank Credit Suisse found the average age of an S&P 500 company is under 20 years, down from 60 years in the 1950s.[1]

Brands can fall out of favour, plant and machinery can fall behind with necessary investment. And all exacerbated by changing trends and nimble upstart competitors. The Fixers are tasked to take radical action to turn things around. An ailing organization might constitute dozens of sites and thousands of staff, but sometimes a single person at the top can make all the difference. Their challenge is to judge it right. There is evidence that corporate surgery can kill the patient, so the surgeon in charge must be careful they don't administer too much shock treatment too soon. They must fashion a fix that will last, not a sticking plaster solution.

Dame Moya had spent those early weeks in 2010 getting to know the Royal Mail, which at the time employed 160,000 staff, delivered 60 million items a day and operated an astonishing 69 mail processing plants. That involved visiting as many places as she could. As unpopular as their decisions might be, Fixers know they have to get the workforce on side. For the most part, it is the long-serving staff who understand why change is so desperately needed in failing businesses. Royal Mail had to slash costs, update working practices and retool itself to become a parcel delivery firm to serve the coming online shopping boom. But to put all that into practice at that moment would have been foolhardy.

'A lot of people say it is all about strategy or vision,' Dame Moya said. 'That may be so for a company not in as much trouble as Royal Mail was in.' For Dame Moya the first challenge was about 'getting your arms around the main business processes and getting them under your control – starting with cash. If you don't start with cash you are going to fall off a cliff. That forces you to look at capital allocation. If there is cash in the till, who has first claim on it?' Cash was always going to play a part in fixing the Royal Mail. The year before Dame Moya arrived, the group had a net trading cash outflow of £517 million, largely because of a giant pension fund contribution of £867 million.

But Fixers are cannier than just ploughing straight in. Two things come up time and again when a new situation presents itself: they do their research before accepting a role and then frame the challenge ahead of them. Only by setting out what success looks like can they be judged to have succeeded – and to be appropriately rewarded for it. Better not to have to fix their own reputation when the assignment is over.

Dame Moya had been courted by Sir Donald Brydon, a veteran asset manager turned City grandee who was Royal Mail's chairman. But she needed to do her own homework about the task at hand. In early 2010, under the guise of an interested overseas business leader, she spoke to Richard Hooper, the former deputy chairman of media regulator Ofcom who had written a review that was published by the government two years earlier recommending private investment in the business. She was cheered to be told that the regulatory model overseeing Royal Mail was totally ineffective and about to implode. But such research only gets you so far. 'You can do a lot of due diligence but you can't really find out what is going on until you get there,' she said. 'There are so many things for which you must take your own temperature, talk to people and listen a lot.'

Then it came to the terms of engagement. Dame Moya worked to understand the art of what was possible. She made it clear that unless the government of the day supported privatization, she was not coming over from Canada. Dame Moya earned her spurs fixing Canada Post, which suffered with many of the same problems as the Royal Mail, except it served half the number of households scattered across an area larger than Europe. She also had experience overturning historical precedent. During her time at Transport Canada, she was heavily involved in privatizing the Canadian National Railway and scrapping the century-old Crow Rate rail subsidy that was used by wheat farmers in the provinces of Saskatchewan and Manitoba to get their crops to market.

Dame Moya wasn't interested in simply getting to grips with another troubled government-owned asset. There had to be a target, an end point. If the shared ambition was to privatize Royal Mail, to make it worth owning by private investors who wouldn't look twice at it at the time, that was a suitable catalyst for modernization and the ultimate fix. This point was resolved on another baking hot after-noon, this time when she was in New York.

In May 2010 Dame Moya was sat in Harvard Yard, the ancient heart of the revered Harvard University, waiting to watch her daughter collect her degree certificate. Just before the graduation ceremony began, her phone rang. It was Sir Donald Brydon calling, with good news and bad news. Her appointment – although she had not at that stage formally accepted the job – was leaking in the media. Sir Donald also read to her from the text of the Queen's Speech confirming that the new coalition government of Conservatives and Liberal Democrats planned to privatize the Royal Mail. 'Count me in,' she said, returning to her seat just in time to witness her daughter's big moment.

So came the cash crunch discovered that August after-noon. Dame Moya got on the phone again, calling her mother, a retired teacher she was very close to whose last-ing lesson to her from childhood had been to speak clearly. Telling her the business she had just taken over was in danger of going bust, the advice down the line from Canada had no less clarity than she expected. Dame Moya recalled being told: 'Whatever plans you had for the weekend, my girl, you better close your door and be ready to go in there on Monday and figure out how that is not going to happen.'

The divorced Dame Moya lived on her own but had had no time yet to find a London home so she retreated to her hotel room to draw up a plan. Fixers are used to hurry-up moments. That makes them the antithesis of many types of leader who like to take their time, to listen and learn, before setting a strategy for their new company to follow. Not for Fixers the corporate phenomenon of effecting change in the first 100 days. Decisive steps must be taken far quicker.

First thing on Tuesday – after the Bank Holiday Monday – Dame Moya gathered her team together to detail her emergency plan which superseded all else she had had in mind. She is charming, opinionated, oh-so-talkative and just a little dramatic: perfectly suited to the ups and downs that lay ahead.

There were three prongs to her emergency plan, she explained to colleagues. Royal Mail had to get some cash in the till urgently, change the payment terms with its suppliers, and, where possible, increase prices. Her first act was to convene a conference for all of Royal Mail's suppliers. She wasn't going to squeeze the little ones. Instead she pleaded for forbearance from the larger ones. She found immediate support from Lord Livingston, at the time the chief executive of BT and Royal Mail's biggest creditor, who agreed she could postpone payments due.

Her tactics were risky. They alerted stakeholders including staff that the Royal Mail was truly in trouble – in truth, most already knew – but also that change was coming and it was being led from the top. This crisis was not to be wasted. Senior staff had no choice but to get behind the new boss, but she was under pressure to deliver.

Dame Moya made clear how solitary the role of a Fixer can be. During those weeks, 'it helped that it was really, really busy,' she said. 'I would work and eat and go to sleep and every now and then go for a long walk, which helps me pick through things that have happened during the day and the signals I was getting. I didn't feel lonely because it was so intense.'

Few Fixers view themselves as merely project managers or caretakers that can walk away from a situation like this. As soon as they have decided to pitch in, they are committed. Nor does the honeymoon period of being the new leader last for long, according to Dame Moya. 'The leverage shifts from the board to the CEO for a period of time, but it is not a long time,' she said. 'Once they have made a decision to put you in the job they can't get rid of you in the first six weeks because it looks like they are a bunch of nitwits. But they can do it seven or eight months in, and for sure after two years.' She didn't have to worry about maintaining board – and government – support. By November that year, suppliers had fallen into line, the cash position had improved and she could breathe a little easier. Now the Fixer could revert to her original plan of action, with the added credibility of someone able to make things happen in an emergency.

No popularity contest

THE year before Dame Moya Greene arrived, Royal Mail might have passed into the hands of CVC Capital Partners, one of the oldest private equity firms in Europe. But the part-privatization deal that had been mooted was delayed by Lord Mandelson, then the Business Secretary, because of political unrest and concern it did not represent good value for taxpayers.

CVC, which already ran postal operations in Belgium and Denmark, was one of the buyout houses that gave birth to a whole new generation of Fixers. These new owners still installed turnaround experts that set out to save businesses, but alongside making operational improvements there was usually a financial restructuring – whether the company needed to overhaul its balance sheet or not. That loaded up the enterprise with debt so a chunky dividend could be drawn by borrowing against future revenue streams. It was a typical tactic as part of squeezing value from underperforming companies. The rest of the playbook was ruthless.

One of CVC's favourite Fixers was Tim Parker, dubbed the 'Prince of Darkness' by angry trade unions for chopping thousands of jobs. Parker made his name – and his nickname – running the UK's Automobile Association, which was part-owned by CVC. Famous for the feats of engineering pulled off by its legion of roadside patrollers when they attend to breakdowns up and down the UK, it didn't take so kindly to having a Fixer planted at the head of the company in 2004.

Under Parker's leadership, the AA's headcount was cut by 3,300 to 6,700 and a refinancing pushed debts up to an eye-watering £1.9 billion. The private equity method drew great controversy. The chairman of the AA's co-owner, the buyout house Permira, was targeted by GMB union activists. Damon Buffini, a regular churchgoer, discovered a camel had been paraded outside his place of worship, Holy Trinity in Clapham, south London, by protestors referencing the biblical saying, 'It is easier for a camel to go through the eye of a needle than for a rich man to enter the kingdom of God'.

The AA wasn't the first time that Parker had souped up a company, having carried out similar turnarounds at family-run shoemaker Clarks and Kwik-Fit, the auto repair chain. Confident, cerebral and laid back, with a mass of grey curls, he was clear that Fixers were rarely in it to be liked. 'I don't love being unpopular, I love to get a job well done and I'm willing to be unpopular,' he said. 'But actually if you go around and ask people what they feel so many years later, they say we did all the right things and we are doing pretty well.'[2] Popularity takes a back seat when you get paid £40 million, as Parker did for his work at the AA.

He was fortunate to see at close quarters how other leaders operated early on in his career. After working as a junior Treasury economist he switched to the private sector. Working as an assistant to Sir William Barlow, the chairman of electricals giant Thorn EMI, was an eye-opener. It also presented him with his big chance when the division he was running, kettle and food mixer manufacturer Kenwood, was earmarked for sale. Parker led a £54 million management buyout in 1989, creating a stake worth £2 million in the float three years later.

That pattern of reviving an unloved and underperforming asset has been repeated many times. For Parker, it runs along these lines: ascertain what is the core operation of a business, strip away anything extraneous, cut costs to free up funds and reinvest those in the core as it is built back up.

His last corporate fix was Samsonite, the luggage company, which was struggling in a severe economic downturn that saw air travel nosedive. Unlike some of his other postings, Samsonite has not been a quick in and out. Parker has been involved since 2008, including five years as chief executive and overseeing the listing of the company's shares in Hong Kong. He reverted to non-executive chairman in autumn 2014. Nor has it been a straight-line recovery – business rarely is.

Parker's style is to be anything but a master of the universe. He could never be confused with an Alpha, for example. Speed matters – and not just because CVC and their ilk are looking to make a quick return. And just like Dame Moya Greene adapting her Royal Mail plan when the money ran out, Parker believes in the power of changing direction.

'The best decisions you can take are when you reverse mistakes,' he said. 'The essence of business is about time and getting things done. The reason a lot of people come unstuck is they become fixated on self-justifying decisions. What I've learnt is I'm not embarrassed if I get something wrong.'[3]

Keeping it simple

MAKING complicated things simple is the hallmark of an effective Fixer. It is something that Sir Christopher Bland understood well. In 2001 he steadied the ship at BT, the former UK telecoms monopoly that had got itself into a terrible mess with a £28 billion debt mountain and sliding sales. As the incoming chairman, Sir Christopher was a big Establishment figure who had already chaired the BBC and numerous private companies.

At the moment of crisis at one of the country's most significant firms, his appointment provided a calming influence and restored some faith among shareholders and staff even before the Fixer got to work. Accentuating the positive and repairing morale is key to any turnaround. 'Who does the research and development for the industry? BT. We do it all – virtually all of it,' he said proudly.[4]

Sir Christopher could have been overwhelmed by the minutiae required to jumpstart a business stifled by bureaucracy that had lingered from its pre-privatization days as a division of the old Post Office. Afraid that its hardy perennial landline income was under threat from the advent of the internet, BT was fighting too many battles. Unperturbed, the former army officer who fenced for Ireland at the 1960 Olympics arrived at BT as if still brandishing his épée to pinpoint priorities.

He boiled down complex problems into a manageable to-do list to focus not just his mind but everyone else's too. Much of the direction of travel had been set by restive investors but Sir Christopher owned these points: demerge the mobile business, sell the Yellow Pages directories unit, launch a bumper rights issue, find a new chief executive. Years later he still carried the list around on a dog-eared scrap of paper, brandishing it every now again and ensuring he was not backward in claiming credit for BT's progress.

Another five 'perpetual challenges' followed, printed on a card he displayed on his desk. They were: growth, defence, customer service, building the network and convincing the government and the regulators of BT's value. Not until 2020, when BT suspended its annual dividend for the first time in 36 years in the wake of the Covid-19 outbreak, had successive leaders been faced with a crisis of the scale of 2001. Nor had they managed to reduce the telecoms firm's mission to such simple and effective terms.

Sometimes Fixers are defined as sector specialists, the last person standing when everyone else around them appears to have been compromised. A Fixer needs a cast-iron reputation if their first act, like Sir Christopher Bland's at BT, is to reassure. Then come the tough decisions.

John McFarlane's return to London from Australia was timely. Not only was his reputation enhanced after a decade down under when he revived Australia and New Zealand Banking Group (ANZ) after stripping back the lender's involvement in emerging markets. In the northern hemisphere, an entire cadre of banking chiefs had not been so fortunate, having lost the faith invested in them either because the institutions they led tumbled into the financial crisis – or because they failed to stagger out again. Senior jobs needed filling and safe pairs of hands were in short supply.

Stocky, self-assured and approachable with a shock of white hair, McFarlane was more than ready to step into the breach. There was a good chance he could have been chairman of the Royal Bank of Scotland, joining the board as a non-executive director soon after the lender's £12 billion rights issue in 2008. The ensuing collapse into state hands after the imperious chief executive Fred Goodwin's reckless acquisition drive changed the dynamics of the role substantially. Clever Fixers are careful about choosing the right berth.

Instead McFarlane emerged in 2012 as chairman at Aviva, the UK's biggest general and life insurer and a sluggish performer that successive managements had failed to get their arms around. What comes up time and again in his way of working is a pattern, as previously described with Tim Parker.

For McFarlane, it starts with the money. Allocate resources where the institution can be distinctive and successful. That means cutting costs and pruning pointless assets in overseas markets that an Alpha leader might cling on to for longer to preserve their empire. No wonder the Scot, who used to perform in a skiffle band called The Sekrets, revelled in the nickname Mack the Knife, a song popularized by 1960s American crooner Bobby Darin.

At Aviva, he got to work immediately, swapping offices with finance chief Pat Regan – who later became chief executive of Australian insurer QBE – so that he didn't have to look out over a construction site. At least Regan was allowed to stay in the building. The chief executive Andrew Moss was forced out by a shareholder revolt. You suspect McFarlane would have helped him out of the door if investors hadn't.

The chairman took temporary charge, formulating a plan within two months while the search for the next chief executive was underway. There would be fewer management layers and 16 out of 58 business units that tied up £6 billion of capital were for the chop. 'I tend to be very intuitive,' he said. 'I don't need to read lots of stuff to work things out, I can get the gist quickly.'[5]

Like Sir Christopher Bland, McFarlane's work is front-loaded. Set the tone and then leave it to his chosen chief executive to pick through the niceties of the action plan. 'There is no way on earth I could conceive of chairing a bank. It is just not possible,' he said in one interview.[6] Just over a year later, in 2015, he was unable to resist the challenge and joined Barclays as chairman.

Here was another sickly institution calling for a firm-handed Fixer. Forget the promise of money: secure in his own abilities, McFarlane was drawn in by a mixture of prestige and adrenalin. On occasion, when he has agreed to a big new role, his wife Anne has to be sweetened with a new piece of jewellery.[7] This sounds like an Alpha tendency, but Fixers do not typically hang around. At Barclays, despite an uneasiness between him and the chief executive Jes Staley, the bank boosted profits but its share price fell and an activist shareholder tried – unsuccessfully – to force the board to downsize the investment banking division.

In April 2020, McFarlane was at it again. He became chairman of Westpac Group, Australia's oldest company and its second-largest retail bank that had been rocked by a money-laundering scandal. They were practically perfect conditions for a veteran Fixer to take control. 'People close to me know that on my return to Australia, I hadn't intended to take another major leadership role,' McFarlane said. 'However, I'm passionate about the Australian banking sector, and I'm excited by the challenge of returning Westpac to its place as a leading global bank, following recent events.'[8]

For a Fixer who became a totem of a turnaround, Tim Parker, John McFarlane and Sir Christopher Bland have nothing on Stephen Hester, the chief executive of Royal Bank of Scotland (RBS) in the aftermath of the 2008 financial crisis when it had required a £45 billion taxpayer bailout. When Ross McEwan took over as chief executive of RBS in 2013, he was presented with a riding hat by his finance director Bruce Van Saun. It was a knowing passing of the baton.

The image of Hester on horseback heading out to hunt foxes coloured the debate over RBS and its revival efforts. Someone togged out like a toff at the helm of the people's bank, majority-owned by the taxpayer, was not a good look. It ensured that Hester became a lightning rod for criticism and for daring to think he deserved to be paid a bonus. For his part, Hester hadn't ridden out since that infamous snap was taken in 2008, before he joined RBS. Not surprisingly, McEwan wasn't about to try the incendiary headgear on for size.

Fixers are often pitched into the eye of the storm and their own well-being can be sacrificed. Hester lost weight and his marriage broke up while leading RBS. If it was just fixing a business, he might have been alright. But the public nature of the rescue – newspaper headlines, questions in Parliament, daily scrutiny – was overwhelming. For a few years, Hester was not just the most high-profile Fixer in the UK, he was the most high-profile chief executive too.

After he was jettisoned by the government in 2013 in a row over strategy, Hester landed almost immediately at RSA, another three-lettered FTSE 100 financial services group in a heap of trouble. It needed fixing but it was small beer compared with RBS, which changed its name to NatWest Group in July 2020. His relief at departing was obvious.

At RBS, government ministers were clear the banker's first and only task was to get the country's money back. But Hester had other priorities. He knew he had to drastically shrink RBS to win back the faith of global money markets and shareholders and customers who were turning their back on the lender after the empire building of his predecessor Goodwin. Eight months on the board of the nationalized Northern Rock could not prepare him for the ordeal he faced. Following a strategic review that set the template for which assets the new RBS would keep and which would be sold, Hester weeded out £3 billion of bad loans in his first three months at the helm and in three years shrank the bank's balance sheet by more than £600 billion.

Moving on in 2014 to general insurer RSA, owner of the More Than brand, speed still mattered. Anyone else might have been overawed by a company that appeared to have run down its financial resources over many years as market conditions declined. Hester's prognosis was all-important. 'The key thing you have to do at the beginning is try to make sure that the underlying company is a good one,' he said, 'because if you supply medicine to a patient with a fatal disease the patient will still die.'[9]

He launched a £773 million rights issue and began a programme of sell-offs to repair a threadbare balance sheet. But like most turnarounds, it promised to be a two-speed process. After fixing the finances it takes much longer to repair reputation, the product offer and trading figures. Hester also had to explain to the 23,000 staff under his leadership why the weather had suddenly changed. That needed to be fast too. But he was sanguine about how honest a Fixer should be with those around them – and when you should move on. 'I think you have to call it how you see it, but equally running a company you have to be a pragmatist,' he said.[10]

Fixed for now

DAME Moya Greene cautions that a Fixer's work is never done. 'If you want to see how fast things can fall apart in this business, look at Canada Post today,' she said in 2013 as her Royal Mail turnaround began bearing fruit. 'After I left they had a national strike and lost a lot of their business.'[11] By this stage, Royal Mail was in better shape: annual profits had almost tripled to £403 million, productivity was up – as was the cost of a first-class stamp, from 46p to 60p – and by October 2013 the company would make its debut on the stock market in a miraculous turn of events.

By the time she stepped down as chief executive in June 2018, Dame Moya's success had come from taming the unions, reducing costs, investing in the business and negotiating an easier regulatory settlement – all the while maintaining a universal service obligation (USO) that meant letters could be delivered six days a week to the Highlands of Scotland for the same price as if they were crossing a few streets in London. Crucially, she persuaded the government to hive off much of the pension commitment that had been draining so much cash from the Royal Mail.

Yet in May 2019, the company's share price was tanking and the dividend was cut. Dame Moya's successor Rico

Back, who had run the group's very profitable European deliveries arm, needed to announce a new turnaround strategy to drive profit margins and boost productivity, promising to plough £1.8 billion into the UK business. By the autumn, the Communication Workers Union that Dame Moya had spent so much time charming was balloting its members on strike action. And in May 2020, with pressure piled on the business by the Covid-19 pandemic and the shares trading at little more than half their flotation price, Back stood down with immediate effect.

The toughest challenge for any Fixer is asking them to prove how successful they have been at restoring a company onto a sustainable footing. It is all very well announcing an aggressive five-point turnaround plan but if it comes to nought they might have been better off not bothering. Leaders who create short-term drama but take no long-term responsibility for the outcome can't be worth recruiting.

A cynical response to that challenge, backed up by so many private equity-inspired turnarounds, is that some fixes are a sticking plaster that works just long enough for the long-term incentive plan to pay out, or as soon as unsuspecting institutional investors have subscribed to shares in the initial public offering. Certainly, the debt burden often introduced by private equity owners can send firms downhill fast if trading does not match forecasts. Dismissing too many staff can wipe out the corporate memory, destroy morale and strip the company of its skills base – metrics that aren't easy to track in the profit and loss account.

The better answer is to say that nothing lasts forever. Auditors trying to justify their existence when an accounting scandal erupts sometimes say the subsequent breakdown of a car cannot be blamed on the last mechanic to repair it if the vehicle has been driven far enough down the road from the garage. If the boss is no longer the boss, whatever problems emerge are not their problem.

Better to travel

Harriet Green was praised for her lightning-quick rescue of Thomas Cook – although that praise faded the closer the UK holiday company came to going bust. It finally succumbed in September 2019, five years after Green's exit, sparking the biggest peacetime repatriation by the Civil Aviation Authority, which was charged with bringing home some 150,000 stranded holidaymakers from sunny climes.

Green's 28 months in charge was certainly a short, sharp shock. It is hard to know whether Thomas Cook would have gone bust sooner if Green had not gone in so hard in an attempt to fix it. Luck and circumstance play a big part in the effectiveness of any leader. Chief executives talk about making the weather but if market conditions are poor – as they soon became in the travel market, just like they were in the deliveries market – the best that can be done is to insulate firms from the worst.

Halfway through Green's time at Thomas Cook, signs of a turnaround were evident and investors were excited. The shares had risen tenfold thanks to swift action to seal a £1.6 billion refinancing, several sell-offs, re-energizing the workforce and identifying £400 million of cost savings as Green sought to prove there was life in the traditional travel agency model when sunseekers found it easy to hunt for bargains online. Investors, customers and the media could see it was full-on.

Green explained she did not like to hang around. Having spent six years at Premier Farnell, a distributor of electronic parts, she was itching for her next role and actually wrote to Thomas Cook's chairman offering her services. 'You sort of know when it's time,' she said, describing when she looked to move on. 'In my case, I know because I am tinkering. The reason for me being there, which is to do profound change, has been embedded.'[12]

For Green, fixing things came from a survival instinct learnt when she worked at Arrow, a highly acquisitive semiconductor distributor. She explained: 'When you land in Korea to fix a business that has just been purchased and your Korean is not that good and it's maybe not the most welcoming environment, you develop a resilience to deal with different cultures and different situations.'[13] She also took tough assignments, such as in sub-Saharan Africa, in a bid to prove herself early on in male-dominated working environments.

Speaking in October 2019 at the Business, Energy and Industrial Strategy Committee's inquiry into Thomas Cook's failure, Green disclosed there had been disagreements about the scale and pace of change at the company that led to her swift departure in November 2014. 'Certainly the board and I had disagreements over the level of assets and over the rate and pace of a digital transformation, which takes daily standing up,' she said. 'This is changing the DNA of a business, just like I did at Premier Farnell, which worked, over a six-year period. We certainly had differences of opinion.'[14]

An ill-judged interview in *The Times* in October 2014 carried out during an early-morning yoga session at her Mayfair hotel (headline: 'How to be a superboss')[15] did not help the mood either. Like Stephen Hester, Green knew it was becoming impossible to do her job when the vital boardroom or shareholder support any Fixer relies on began to ebb away.

Where Fixers differ from Alphas is that they ultimately have far less power. They are hired to save a company but when the immediate danger has passed, boards seeking an easier life can choose to find a leader less hard-driving and less likely to rock the boat.

Nor does the corporate shock treatment always work. But because companies are forever getting themselves into trouble, someone has to try. What is clear from the Royal Mail example is that Fixers have a role to play but to declare a company ever truly fixed is a dangerous game. It carries on developing, trading and competing as if it is a living entity. The failure to keep the trade unions onside might suggest a fragile legacy but ultimately it is a responsibility passed on as soon as Dame Moya Greene has left the building.

Despite their fearsome reputation that they do much to stoke, it is plain that Fixers are not always effective. But catalysts for change are essential for struggling companies. The alternative would be for them never to collapse into crisis in the first place. This might be called perpetual fixing.

There is a good example of this style of leadership at Diageo. When the modest Indian-born Ivan Menezes succeeded Paul Walsh at the helm of the gin-to-Guinness drinks combine in 2013 it wasn't clear the company needed fixing at all. Walsh had been a big game hunter in private but also in public thanks to the giant acquisitions he sealed to vault the company into the consumer big league. The balance sheet was strong and end-markets were healthy. Diageo was even getting on top of what was expected of it by the responsible drinking lobby.

But the switch happened at just the right time. Menezes quietly made the company run better, focusing on its premium brands including Johnnie Walker whisky, Ciroc vodka and Tanqueray gin, selling the luxury Scottish hotel Gleneagles for £200 million, delayering management and pouring millions more into marketing. This type of perpetual fix, an ongoing cycle of operational improvement, is the kind of relentless tinkering of which Harriet Green said she was easily bored.

Simply running businesses better has to be the ambition of every corporate leader but if they all succeeded Fixers would be out of a job. Many external factors, ebbs and flows, luck and judgement mean that that will never happen. After all, no chief executive sets out to run a business badly. What Fixers excel at is framing the challenge, following the money, setting a narrative for staff and suppliers to buy into, and then acting on it as best they can, at speed. But one three-year – or three-month – strategy must lead to another. A company cannot drift along, but nor can it be placed on a permanent war footing. Life after fixing demands another type of leader.

FIXERS IN BRIEF

Strengths: Fast, fearless, straightforward, unpopular (or totemic morale boosters!).

Weaknesses: Short-termist, risk-taking, ruthless.

Suitability: Crisis situations, reviving serial underperforming companies.

Where you will find them: Taking the helm somewhere when all hope is lost.

Endnotes

This chapter: original Dame Moya Greene interview

1 CreditSuisse (2017) Global equity themes. https://plus.credit-suisse.com/rpc4/ravDocView?docid=_XHwk2AL-YxKG (archived at https://perma.cc/9ZJV-AX92)

2 Ashton, J (2013) From shoes to luggage, it's another open and shut case for Samsonite's Tim Parker, *Evening Standard*, 3 May. https://www.standard.co.uk/business/markets/from-shoes-to-luggage-it-s-another-open-and-shut-case-for-samsonites-tim-parker-8602313.html (archived at https://perma.cc/PVG9-SNHE)

3 Ibid.

4 Ashton, J (2004) BT's rugged champion proves he is master of the cut and thrust, *Daily Mail*, 17 June

5 Ashton, J (2013) Music man John McFarlane is calling the tune at the House of the Rising Funds Aviva, *Evening Standard*, 1 November. https://www.standard.co.uk/business/markets/music-man-john-mcfarlane-is-calling-the-tune-at-the-house-of-the-rising-funds-aviva-8917234.html (archived at https://perma.cc/HRL6-T4ER)

6 Ibid.

7 Financial Review (2020) Inside McFarlane's Westpac rescue plan, 24 January. https://www.afr.com/chanticleer/inside-mcfarlane-s-westpac-rescue-plan-20200123-p53u3p (archived at https://perma.cc/MNH7-MBXT)

8   Westpac (2020) Westpac announces John McFarlane as incoming
    Chairman [Online Media Release] 23 January. https://www.westpac.
    com.au/about-westpac/media/media-releases/2020/23-january/
    (archived at https://perma.cc/PAP8-G6H3)

9   Ashton, J (2014) Interview: RSA Group chief executive Stephen
    Hester – A banking blow-up and gardening leave: What Mr Fix-It did
    next, *Evening Standard*, 4 July. https://www.standard.co.uk/business/
    markets/interview-rsa-group-chief-executive-stephen-hester-a-banking-
    blow-up-and-gardening-leave-what-mr-fix-9584169.html (archived at
    https://perma.cc/ESE8-6BBU)

10 Ibid.

11 Ashton, J (2013) Royal Mail's Moya Greene has sorted profits but can
    she deliver on the stock market too? *Evening Standard*, 24 May.
    https://www.standard.co.uk/business/markets/royal-mails-moya-greene-
    has-sorted-profits-but-can-she-deliver-on-the-stock-market-
    too-8630581.html (archived at https://perma.cc/XE2W-LD8E)

12 Ashton, J (2013) Buckle up, says Harriet Green, the jetset boss of
    Thomas Cook with no time to loll on the sun lounger, *Evening
    Standard*, 20 September. https://www.standard.co.uk/business/markets/
    buckle-up-says-harriet-green-the-jetset-boss-of-thomas-cook-with-no-
    time-to-loll-on-the-sun-lounger-8829118.html (archived at https://
    perma.cc/YHP6-FHY5)

13 Ibid.

14 Business, Energy and Industrial Strategy Committee (2019) Oral
    Evidence: Thomas Cook, HC 39, House of Commons, 23 October.
    http://data.parliament.uk/writtenevidence/committeeevidence.svc/
    evidencedocument/business-energy-and-industrial-strategy-committee/
    thomas-cook/oral/106595.html (archived at https://perma.cc/
    KL6D-8SNX)

15 Whitworth, D (2014) Harriet Green: How to be a superboss, *The
    Times*, 18 October. Available at https://www.thetimes.co.uk/article/
    harriet-green-how-to-be-a-superboss-67n9bg97jnb (archived at https://
    perma.cc/L24M-79UZ)

CHAPTER THREE

Sellers

The consumer drug

For a three-month period in 1977, an eager young man with a curious accent drove from clinic to clinic all over Columbus, the state capital of Ohio in the Midwestern United States.

He was one of a legion of so-called 'detail men', dispatched by pharmaceuticals companies to impart information about their latest treatments in the hope the doctor they were pitching to would prescribe them to his or her patients.

Sat quietly next to patients in the waiting room, his type was smartly dressed in a suit and often a trilby. They bided their time in anticipation of either an appointed slot or a few minutes snatched with the physician when they came up for air. When their moment came, they might remember birthdays, remonstrate over the performance of the local baseball team, or ask after the doctor's family. And then their patter might extend to the latest drug that had come onto the market or new reports just published about its efficacy.

To 'carry the bag' remains a badge of honour in the world of pharmaceuticals, even though physicians get their drug information from many sources today and scepticism has grown towards giving time over to sales representatives. Still, the link between grass roots communication and shifting cases of product is not broken. The bag, never far from the feet of the detail man – or sometimes woman – contains the tools of the trade much as it did in the 1970s: drug samples, research articles and pens, pads and mugs. These giveaways emblazoned with product logos were designed to embed this particular treatment in the physician's mind long after the detail man had departed for his next meeting.

Along with the bag came a car, an expense account, and a bonus, as long as sales quotas were met. Driving from meeting to meeting could be a lonely existence. There could be rejection, but it was enervating for the most part. Think the opposite of the exhausted, failing Willy Loman in Arthur Miller's play *Death of a Salesman*. This particular Columbus sales representative learnt to think on his feet and the importance of grasping the facts. It was an interlude in a momentous career that would stand him in good stead. Rather than an ordinary foot soldier living the American Dream, in another 21 years he would be leading the corporation whose bag he carried in and out of doctors' surgeries day after day.

By 1998 the Moroccan-born Sidney Taurel, whose French accent marked him out from many other Ohioan detail men and was a talking point in those early physician meetings, would be surveying the globe from an executive floor in Indianapolis, a three-hour drive west of Columbus. It is there that Eli Lilly, the drugs giant best known for bringing the anti-depressant Prozac to the world, is based.

'When you are really good you are a consultant to the physician,' said Taurel, recalling those months as a sales-person many years later. 'You bring your expert knowledge of the product. You need to do that with respect for his or her medical expertise – but they don't know as much about the product as the sales reps do.' Taurel was six years into his Eli Lilly career when he was dispatched to learn to sell. His early grounding was in marketing, with postings in Brazil and Eastern Europe.

Those twin disciplines – sales and marketing – are two sides of the same coin. One attempts to open the conversation with the customer through engaging campaigns and brand building. The other aims to close the conversation by completing the transaction, aided by market intelligence and product knowledge. Sales and marketing are united in their ambition to finesse the message, grow the top line and outpace the competition.

The other thing that unites them is that these disciplines didn't use to create so many leaders. Information technology and computing were exceptions, where the product was a complicated, big-ticket purchase in a fast-changing industry. It partly explains the ascent of Ginni Rometty at IBM, Steve Ballmer at Microsoft and former eBay and Hewlett-Packard boss Meg Whitman. But now look. There are numerous notable Sellers that have made it to the top in many industries. A whole host of executives began their careers promoting soap or snacks at consumer goods giants Unilever and Procter & Gamble – of which more later.

The rise of Sellers as prolific leaders is a modern phenomenon. It tallies with many countries' switch to a service economy, the decline in manufacturing and the liberalization of formerly state-run utilities that drove new competition. Given the demand of always-on media and greater reputational risk, communication skills have become a must-have. Those leaders with an innate sense of connecting with the customer and promoting their wares to them have the edge over many others. They are presentable, confident and persuasive. And in building high-flying careers, Sellers are also good at selling themselves.

The medicine man

Eli Lilly was built on sales. The company was founded in 1876 by Colonel Lilly, a pharmaceutical chemist and veteran of the US Civil War who was frustrated by the ineffective medicines of the day. Early successes included mass-producing the polio vaccine and insulin. But the drugs industry pioneers that included Eli Lilly soon realized that developing great product was nothing without developing great routes to market too.

'Selling is of course a *sine qua non* condition but you also must have a good knowledge of the product and be really very objective in the way you present both the pluses and the minuses – and don't try to oversell,' said Taurel, who joined the firm as a marketing associate in 1971 after studying at the École des Hautes Études Commerciales in Paris and receiving an MBA from Columbia University in New York. 'What I also learned was how isolated a job this is. You have to be a self-starter, and a self-motivator.'

Taurel had little time to build the years-long relationships with physicians and their administrative staff that sustained many of his fellow salespeople in their life on the road. Later in 1977 he tried his hand as a district manager coordinating a team of salespeople. It was all in preparation for a more senior role in his ascent of the company. At the age of 28, Taurel soon switched back across the Atlantic to be sales director in France – where he had studied less than a decade before – with a team of 150 people beneath him.

Today, he is erudite, expansive, tanned, relaxed and still in demand, chairing the UK education group Pearson since 2016 and sitting on the board of IT giant IBM since 2001.

He went on: 'The pharmaceutical industry is a high-risk, high-margin industry. The value of each customer is so high.' It explains why so much is spent on cultivating and keeping each of them. In the 1970s, through opinion panels and analysis of sales data, the pharmaceuticals industry was way ahead of many other industries in understanding consumer needs and arming its salespeople accordingly. Eli Lilly had a good handle on doctors' habits and it could cross-check their behaviour with information gathered from the drugstores. This helped the firm to target the most important physician in each region – the one who saw the most patients, wrote the most prescriptions and might be expected to influence others in the locality.

In addition, a huge amount of work went into understanding how Eli Lilly's product fitted in with all the other resources at the physician's disposal and their pros and cons. When Taurel was briefly in sales, group products included the antibiotic Keflex and Dobutrex, a heart drug. Along with drug development, it is a discipline that goes right to the heart of the company.

'The two key factors are successful science that addresses unmet medical needs and then good marketing efforts to ensure those products are being appropriately used by physicians,' he added. The generous margins meant that salesforces did not need to keep a close watch on what they were spending. 'There was relatively little need for much effort on cost cutting and being really efficient, so the industry was happy for a very long time. It has changed now.'

It begs the question of what skills a Seller has to deploy when selling is not enough. Organizations with strong brands should be able to sustain higher margins than ones with weak brands that must slash prices to win market share. But there are times when sales are not rising inexorably and competition bites.

Sellers need more than polished sales patter and slick marketing to thrive in leadership roles. They must broaden their range to fix strategy and control costs. This test of versatility involves the biggest promotional challenge of them all: marketing themselves to chairmen and shareholders as the complete leadership package.

The Proctoid takeover

It was Gavin Patterson's cricket jumper that first caught the eye. The future chief executive of BT, the UK's leading telecoms company, was picking his way through the bustling careers fair at Cambridge University in November 1989 when someone shouted over, 'Do you play cricket?'

Despite his sartorial elegance, Patterson didn't. But instead of ambling past another stand promoting an employer that was in town to lure the brightest and best onto its graduate scheme, he stopped to chat and a career was born.

So was a friendship. In a remarkable piece of fate, staffing the Procter & Gamble stand that day was a young man called Philip Jansen. Almost 30 years later, in February 2019, Jansen would succeed Patterson in leading BT.

They are not the only ones to roll off the Pampers-to-Pringles leadership production line. Over the course of a golden decade, the US groceries giant spawned a remarkable number of Sellers both in the UK and internationally. That P&G trained its recruits with a foundation in sales and marketing helps to explain how they were turned into leadership material.

The roll-call of leaders is certainly impressive. From selling shampoo and deodorant, P&G alumni have run companies that tout luxury cars, clothing, broadband, insurance and pay-TV. But rather than swapping one product line for – usually – a more expensive one, they have rounded themselves out to become in-demand chief executives, instead of salesmen or chief marketers.

Naples-born Fabrizio Freda was made chief executive of make-up and fragrance group Estée Lauder in 2009, having joined P&G in 1982 and risen to become president of its global snacks division. Patrice Louvet, appointed chief executive of Ralph Lauren in 2017, began his career in P&G's marketing department in France in 1989 and gained early experience in haircare. Allison Kirkby, who spent 20 years at P&G up until 2010, became chief executive of Scandinavian telecoms provider Telia in 2020 and also sits on the BT board as a non-executive director. Chris de Lapuente joined luxury goods house LVMH in 2011 as chief executive of Sephora and later took responsibility for many of the group's perfume and cosmetics brands. He began at P&G in 1983 and in 2004 rose to become its youngest president, in charge of haircare.

The list of P&G Sellers goes on: Stefan Bomhard was poached from luxury car distributor Inchcape in 2020 to run tobacco group Imperial Brands, Chip Bergh led jeans maker Levi Strauss from 2011, Chris Pilling was in charge of the Yorkshire Building Society from 2012 to 2016, and John Hardie ran news provider ITN until 2018 after nearly a decade in charge. As for Patterson, in July 2020 he became president and chief revenue officer of Salesforce, the fast-growing US cloud software company, taking leadership of the company's global sales organization.

There is something about spending formative years at the consumer sharp end that stands executives in good stead. Working as a salesman on the frontline can be character forming – which is another way of saying that it can be a hard slog. Andy Cosslett made his name running Holiday Inn owner Intercontinental Hotels Group after 14 years at Cadbury Schweppes. He also took the helm of Fitness First, the gym chain that had been through a debt restructuring and was suffering from falling membership. But he still recalled his Unilever years proudly.

The chairman of Rugby Football Union since 2016 and from 2017 Kingfisher, the owner of the B&Q home improvements chain, when he started out Cosslett toured the corner shops of Liverpool in the depths of winter. As a sales representative for Wall's ice-cream, selling sand to the Arabs might have been easier. But it taught him perseverance – and also to question the findings of customer surveys. 'I remember research that said no man would pay more than 50p for an ice cream and they wouldn't hold anything with a stick,' he said. 'Then you look at the success of Magnum.'[1] That's the power of marketing and sales.

Founded in 1837, P&G has always been the company where product meets promotion. One of its first brands, Ivory soap, invented by James Gamble, owes much of its success to how it was marketed by Harley Procter as the revolutionary soap that floats in the bath. That was a handy characteristic when people were washing in murky rivers. To add gloss to its sales pitch, Ivory was sent to college chemistry professors to validate its lack of impurities.

Fast forward 150 years and P&G's high strike rate in producing Sellers has much to do with the premium it placed on marketing, plus the type of people it recruited in the first place. Gavin Patterson had an eye out for the company before he was spotted by Jansen that day in 1989 at the careers fair. He had been looking for 'the best business education I could find'.

Patterson was a university entrepreneur, setting up while studying a market research firm called Cambridge Surveys that canvassed the student body on various issues, mainly linked to recruitment. He was already selling. Rather than consumer goods, his product offered access to what was on the minds of the Cambridge University populace. Patterson even linked up with the trail-blazing polling company Gallup.

'I made quite a bit of money,' he said, recalling those days in 2019. 'I concluded I really enjoyed doing that but I felt I needed to learn how to do it more professionally.'

Patterson wasn't the only P&G-er with experience of turning a profit. Tim Davie, the BBC's director-general from September 2020, marketed Vidal Sassoon shampoo and Insignia body spray at P&G. Prior to that he ran club nights while at Cambridge with Christian Tattersfield, who went on to become the boss of Warner Music UK. John Vincent, the co-founder of healthy fast-food chain Leon, put on similar events at the same university with Richard Reed, one of the brains behind Innocent smoothies, before spending four years at P&G.

In the late 1980s, UK companies with an entrepreneurial spirit were thin on the ground. Fittingly for a company that prized the power of marketing, P&G made sure it stood out by advertising heavily in student media with eye-catching slogans such as 'We will teach you how to run a business at 25'. It is notable that the marketing discipline wasn't so much part of its marketing pitch, even though it would make up much of the work that successful candidates were tasked with. P&G also used recent recruits – such as Jansen – to sell the firm's merits to the next intake, often sending them back to their alma mater to do so.

How many each brought in was a source of competitive pride. Such tactics bred an early camaraderie among Proctoids. That was the nickname given to members of the youthful army that baffled their student peers by enthusing about the relative merits of different brands of washing-up liquid and the best sales techniques.

Learning to sell

And then there is what they actually learnt. Accepting no more than 15 marketing candidates each year – with a similar programme running in sales – P&G's was a prized graduate scheme that permitted great freedom within a rigid structure. After drumming up interest at careers fairs, a vacation course took place at Christmas in the students' final academic year. Prospective joiners could learn some of the basics before signing on the line and P&G could watch them in action and sift out the stragglers. There was another split, between the north and south of England. P&G ran major sites at Gosforth outside Newcastle and Egham in Surrey, where Patterson reported for duty after a spell of travelling.

On day one in September, new starters were straight away assigned to a brand that swiftly took over their lives. Often it was a decades-old name, but the newcomers were invited to think about what it meant to them and the relationship with the product's long-time customer base. Patterson was allocated Old Spice aftershave for his first year before he was moved into haircare. Who got what was fairly random but everyone was rotated onto something else no more than 18 months later. It is a minor detail, but those rotations were controlled at a higher level to overcome the natural stasis that persists lower down many organizations.

'To really develop people you need to move them around without their line managers interfering,' Patterson said. 'You like to think they've got your long-term interests at heart but if you're very good your boss will never let you go.'

P&G was peculiar because not only did it favour promoting from within, it was a US company that relied almost solely on local talent in the UK instead of expats. For strong performers, that meant progress was brisk. From the position of assistant brand manager for three years, recruits would be made up to brand manager. In two or three assignments over five years the twentysomethings developed marketing plans, product packaging and advertising promotions. Data was married with creativity. There was little they didn't know about the goods that lined supermarket shelves, including how each brand ranked against the competition. Plenty of time was spent thinking about strategy and the customer, through focus groups and quantitative market research. There was lots of interplay with other internal functions. Because each brand was run independently in each country, with 80 per cent of decisions taken on the ground, it often felt like running a mini company within a company.

Two years in, Patterson was already enjoying the weight of responsibility. He was a senior brand manager on Wash & Go shampoo, whose memorable advertising campaign ran: 'Take two bottles into the shower? Not me! I just want to wash my hair and go.' Patterson's boss left and his boss went on maternity leave. For a year he operated without the two layers of management above him and P&G was happy to let him get on with commissioning advertising and signing off cheques for £1 million a time to pay for media space in newspapers and on TV.

'In many ways, it is not a marketing job in a traditional sense of the word,' he said. 'From a year or two in you are managing the profitability of a brand of which marketing is seen to be the key demand driver.' Patterson had already been moved into a European role before a promotion to become Pantene's marketing director in 1994. The brand was a relative newcomer to the P&G portfolio, having been picked up via acquisition. However, it was growing rapidly and had become the company's third biggest brand overall.

'P&G was an unusual place by giving early responsibility to people,' said Paul Geddes, another of Patterson's peers, who went on to run insurer Direct Line after managing Max Factor and Fairy Non Bio washing powder in his early years. He added: 'It gave 23-year-olds brands and factories and if they had an idea they would pretty much say to you go and do it.' Geddes praised that stance for what it did for individuals. 'I think that is something we all have to take into our own businesses. If you are given some good training in a good situation it is amazing what you can do with those early breaks and that early confidence.'

But looking back he questions whether it was the best business model. 'What it meant is that every market had different plans and products so it was a bit inefficient. Now it is probably not the way they run their business.'[2]

Things did change towards the end of the 1990s. A new UK beauty headquarters was built in Weybridge seven miles away, while Egham largely became a research and development site. The plum marketing jobs that carried profit and loss responsibility across Europe – including those that had been run from Egham and Gosforth – were gradually moved to Geneva.

The changes hastened some of P&G's best operators out of the door. By this time Patterson was marketing director of haircare for Europe. 'I was all set to go to Geneva and then the realization sank in. I was probably leaving the UK for good because the way they were reconfiguring the business, the only job above me was the UK general manager.' He thought he had a slim chance of ever landing that role. Given he and his wife Karen were starting a family, he didn't want to get on the international treadmill that Sidney Taurel so relished at Eli Lilly. In 1999, after nine years at the firm, he quit. Almost all of his peers from the 1990 intake had already gone.

Announced in 1998, Organization 2005 was a new company structure designed to drive faster innovation at P&G. In truth, it standardized much of the activity in which the Patterson cohort had thrived. It presaged a period of crisis for the company, perhaps the worst in its 183-year history.

But it did not last long. The arrival of AG Lafley as chief executive in June 2000 led to a remarkable growth spell. In the following five years, P&G increased sales by more than 40 per cent, doubled profits, generated more than $30 billion in free cash flow and delivered more than $70 billion in shareholder value.

Investors were satisfied. But perhaps P&G's biggest contribution to the UK economy had occurred in the previous decade, when it launched the careers of dozens of future leaders. By the time Lafley had sent sales soaring, most of these super sales and marketing men – and a handful of women – had departed the company, on their way to finding a boardroom of their own.

Mike Clasper, the former chief executive of the British Airports Authority who since 2020 has chaired SSP, the airport and railway station caterer, was several years ahead of Patterson at P&G. He recalled 'a place of intense career rivalry yet day-to-day collaboration' where winning awards for talked-about advertising campaigns became highly prized. That collaboration translated into a tight network of executives who still meet regularly, compare career notes and spur each other on. The success of this club, hand-picked from a narrow set of universities, knocks the theory that diverse teams lead to better outcomes. But it does prove the notion that early responsibility generates an appetite for more – and the confidence to go out and get it.

Echoing the approach that worked for Ivory soap all those years ago, Clasper added: 'In P&G, there are two fundamental drivers of success, the quality and innovation in the products and the creation and exploitation of great brands. Hence, the "hero" functions are marketing and research and development. Of these, it is the marketers more than any other group that are groomed for general management. This is not the case for most companies.' So these Sellers, groomed to emerge from the marketing function – and to some extent sales – might have outrun the organization even if it hadn't been reorganized.

What came next was fortuitous. The executives who were there regard the fast-moving consumer goods (FMCG) industry in the 1990s with misty-eyed nostalgia. It was regularly front-page news, until the internet grabbed the headlines. Early search engines and e-commerce were in vogue; selling toothpaste was not. But broadly, businesses had to work harder to chase customers presented with new distractions.

'A lot of us went into telecoms and media because those industries wanted to become more consumer-oriented,' Patterson said. 'If you wanted to find people in the City that had consumer-first wired into their DNA there were only two places to go: P&G and Unilever.'

The marketing techniques learnt at both of those firms have fanned out across a range of industries. At Sky, the chief executive since 2007, Jeremy Darroch, oversaw a clever exercise in market segmentation when the satellite broadcaster introduced low-cost sister service Now TV in 2012. There are obvious parallels with the 'ladders' of brands Darroch got to know at P&G, where he worked on Clearasil skin cream and Vicks VapoRub. The company was a past master at capturing customers with the cheapest, entry-level goods, such as soap powder brand Daz Automatic, in the hope it might one day persuade them to trade up to the more expensive Ariel. The same is true of the family of insurance brands that Geddes operated at Direct Line.

More than a marketer

Despite the increasing number of chief executives to have originated from sales and marketing backgrounds, few of them want to be defined by it. It is one string to their bow, and by the time they have ascended to chief executive, not the most important one. This stance is diametrically opposite to bosses such as Lord Browne of Madingley, who led BP until 2007. In a profession crying out for an influx of talent, he is eager to stand up and be counted as an engineer.

Sellers may be reluctant to be known for a function historically regarded as lightweight when compared with accountancy, the law or science. Or perhaps crafting that marketing campaign or developing a new sales channel was so long ago they would rather leave it behind. Either way, there is an irony that the marketing discipline is fertile ground for future leaders but has an image problem among senior corporate ranks.

Dave Lewis reached a crucial point in his career in summer 2014. That was when he started work as chief executive of British supermarket group Tesco, which was undergoing as much of a crisis as a market-leading giant ever has. Lewis was going from being a divisional chief at Unilever – albeit a huge division with haircare brands including TRESemmé and Toni & Guy, which if carved out would have entered the FTSE 100 in its own right – to lead one of the UK's best-known companies.

Tesco was reeling from a second profits warning, its dividend had been chopped, and an accounts black hole had been discovered. The group that had relentlessly dominated the UK grocery market for a generation, expanding into telecoms and banking, had declared the space race was over. Big box retailers could no longer keep opening new stores to boost sales. They needed to do something else to carry on growing.

Lewis appeared to be a typical Seller: clean-cut, fast-talking, honest, supremely confident, dressed down in white shirt and dark jeans. At this juncture he was also keen to promote his talents. Taking on Tesco was a daunting prospect, but Lewis wasn't afraid to underline his own breadth of experience. 'One of the things I have loved from the favelas in Brazil to the islands of Java is getting that connection with consumers,' he said.[3]

Going through the facts also meant correcting a few misconceptions. Lewis launched Dove soap in the UK in 1992 – which grew to become one of Unilever's biggest brands – but he didn't create Dove's Real Beauty campaign for which he has been so often credited. The campaign was a runaway success. It began with a sponsored exhibition of work by female photographers including Annie Leibovitz in Toronto. Aided by market research that found only 2 per cent of women considered themselves beautiful, Unilever led the conversation that explored self-loathing and the path to empowerment.

Lewis made it plain he was already above such work, steering clear of the Cannes Lions advertising festival where his division had picked up a hatful of awards over the years. However, he was still proud that he created the environment that let his team do great creative work. In contrast, he was much more relaxed about the label 'Drastic Dave', which emerged in the trade media after he had led a no-holds-barred restructuring at Unilever's UK division when sales fell off a cliff. No surprise there. He would need to be every bit as drastic to get Tesco into shape, which, by the time he departed in 2020, he had done.

It was not cute marketing that was going to do that for him. Part of his success was sales-led, however, because Lewis injected some life into the moribund UK stores that were suffering at the hands of cut-price competitors Aldi and Lidl. But his rescue was also structural and strategic – spinning off overseas assets and acquiring wholesaler Booker – and cultural, once he forged warmer relations with suppliers that had regarded Tesco as the enemy for many years. Lewis the Seller had developed into the full package.

Stevie Spring offered a similar response soon after she arrived as chairman of the British Council in 2019. The state-supported organization is the UK's main tool for cultural outreach, organizing everything from art exhibitions to English language training around the world in the name of good international relations. It employs 12,000 people in more than 100 countries. How appropriate, then, for someone with a background in advertising to be leading the UK's soft power push, especially as Brexit became a reality.

Spring was as bright and engaging as ever and delighted she had landed the role after initially being convinced the headhunter only wanted her on the shortlist for the sake of diversity. But she protested at being pigeonholed for one activity because she had not worked in advertising – in agencies such as Young & Rubicam, Grey Group and Gold

Greenlees Trott – for two decades. It was a fair point. But like any seasoned Seller she went on to demonstrate she still knew the impact of a good campaign. 'The more you know, the more you trust, the higher the propensity to come and be educated here or do business here,' she said.[4]

The former Direct Line chief executive Paul Geddes – who since 2019 has led UK digital education firm QA – expanded on the subject of what he carried over from the P&G years into broader leadership. 'Some things map over quite well,' he said. 'A lot of the job of CEO is communication; another key job is understanding the market and the customer. Ultimately the CEO is chief marketer. Having someone whose skillset is to weigh up all the priorities in favour of what the customer cares about is a good skillset.'[5] So marketing is a major discipline. Sellers just have to pick up everything else along the way – and deal with criticism that marketing alone does not prepare them for the top job.

Questions were raised when Tim Davie was shifted from marketing to run the BBC's vast radio arm in 2008. How on earth was the man who masterminded a relaunch of Pepsi by turning the Daily Mirror's red-top masthead blue for the day qualified to oversee cultural gems such as *The Archers* and The Proms? His answer in spring 2014, having moved the previous year into a subsequent role, heading the corporation's commercial arm BBC Worldwide, was that: 'If it's a new territory people always ask questions. There is only ever one way to deal with that and that is to deliver in the job.'[6] In 2020, Davie was handed the ultimate opportunity to deliver when he was made director-general of the BBC.

The fact is that becoming a marketing success is often a passport out of the marketing department. Sales is no different. Martina King is a seasoned executive who since 2012 has run Featurespace, a Cambridge University fintech start-up that combats credit card crime. Her early career was spent in sales – telephone sales with *The Observer* and then classified advertising at *The Guardian*, where she overlapped with future ITV boss Dame Carolyn McCall. That led her to Capital Radio, when the station ruled London and disc jockey Chris Tarrant was waking up half of the city with his unmissable breakfast show. King's job was to persuade advertisers that commercial radio did not deserve its downmarket reputation. She did so – and in 1993 was promptly switched into general management to run all of Capital's London stations.

'I advise everybody to do sales,' King said. 'It is such an important skill set to have and it doesn't matter what sector you are in. It teaches you so much about being able to build a business.'[7]

Geddes was also promoted and his defining leadership task began in 2009. He had to carve the car and home insurance business Direct Line out from the Royal Bank of Scotland, a transaction forced by European regulators as the price of the bank's taxpayer bailout following the financial crisis. It hadn't looked as though Direct Line would be a stock market hit but Geddes proved the critics wrong by working harder a portfolio of insurance brands: Direct Line, Churchill, Privilege, Green Flag and so on. In the run-up to that point he had worked hard to fill in the gaps on his CV.

'Obviously there are many things the marketer doesn't inherently know how to do or things that may pull in different directions,' he said. 'That means I think you have to deliberately say here's the stuff which people wouldn't expect of a marketer or a marketer wouldn't know how to do and you then need to work assiduously to convince people you can do the other stuff. I probably spent several years not focusing on marketing at all because that wasn't the chief challenge of the business at that time and I also needed to show people I could do the other parts of the job.'[8]

Selling up

By the time Sidney Taurel became chief executive of Eli Lilly in July 1998, he had successfully broadened his skillset too. When he returned to Brazil as general manager in 1981, finance was crucial. In the group's agricultural division, the nine months of credit offered to Brazilian farmers to match the crop cycle was judged unsustainable. Because of the chronic inflation that was plaguing the country at that time and a rash of copycat products flooding the market, Taurel had to recalculate terms.

It was just as well he was ready to tackle all eventualities as chief executive, because Taurel's predecessor Randall Tobias left huge shoes to fill. In his five-year reign, Tobias had overseen a five-fold increase in the company's stock market value, outperforming all of its sector peers. He had streamlined the company, spinning out its medical devices arm, Guidant Corporation.

Taurel's decade in charge of Eli Lilly was defined by a tougher environment. Prozac was 30 per cent of group sales when he took over so he had to invest in research and development to diversify the product pipeline. But the company had to run faster as cheaper generic versions of its drugs came to market. Prozac lost US patent protection in 2001 and costs had to be cut.

Powering sales forward was hugely important, as long as the company had enough products to sell. On Taurel's watch, Eli Lilly pushed through a slew of new drug launches and was positioned well in growing markets such as cancer. That was no mean feat, given that the time it took to get new drugs approved was lengthening. If marketing and sales shone through in Taurel's role, it was the way in which he became an elder statesman for the industry as it navigated regulatory and political pressure. He successfully argued that price controls dampened product development by Big Pharma firms which deserved high returns for making long-term investments.

Eli Lilly also overreached itself. In early 2009, the year after Taurel stood down, the company agreed to pay $1.4 billion in a settlement with the US Justice Department for marketing its bestselling anti-psychotic drug Zyprexa for unapproved applications. In the later years of his leadership, Taurel's priority had been on creating a sense of purpose in the company that meant prolonging and saving lives, not merely selling.[9]

Sat in his office adorned with a giant, wall-mounted television and two framed Liverpool FC shirts, Gavin Patterson explained how BT would find some growth after years of a depressed top line. By spending BT's money on broadcasting rights to top-flight football he wanted the telecoms provider to offer an alternative to the free broadband with which pay-TV giant Sky – run by his former

P&G colleague and neighbour Darroch – was trying to entice subscribers.

With better product and better marketing, this Seller succeeded where his predecessors had failed. The acquisition of mobile firm EE – unwinding a move that had taken BT out of the mobile market years earlier – was also a big hit. Where life became harder was with the regulatory battles over BT's Openreach access division and an Italian accounting scandal that laid the shares low and tested investors' faith.

Patterson's P&G background has provided a solid bedrock for his career but also something of a frustration. Even when he exited BT after 15 years in 2019, having left P&G in 1999, the *Daily Mail* still labelled Patterson as a 'soap suds salesman'. Selling and marketing were at the root of some – but not all – of his smartest moves. Somewhat ironically, the critics who called for an engineer to be put in charge of BT couldn't see the one right under their nose. Back at Cambridge, the day he was enticed to join P&G by Philip Jansen, Patterson had been studying for a degree in engineering.

What is clear is that Sellers have earned their place in the boardroom. The sales discipline gets future leaders in front of the consumer early on. Done properly, marketing should get them into the mind of a consumer. Both skills remain invaluable, especially for grocery companies now struggling to keep track of what consumers want. That arguably makes the corporate marketer and salesperson who can reach the social media-influenced shopper in search of small batch, organic, low-fat, local produce even smarter than those that went before. And – having broadened out their skills base – if they can do the same at the helm of pharmaceuticals, telecoms and luxury goods companies, all the better.

SELLERS IN BRIEF

Strengths: Customer insightful, communicative, competitive, clear-sighted.

Weaknesses: Perceived as lacking in other disciplines such as finance and strategy.

Suitability: Consumer-facing, fast-changing, price-driven industries.

Where you will find them: Everywhere there is a consumer good to sell or relationship to develop. So everywhere really.

Endnotes

This chapter: original Sidney Taurel, Gavin Patterson, Mike Clasper interviews

1 Ashton, J (2013) A fresh health kick for Fitness First boss Andy Cosslett who's flexing his corporate muscle, *Evening Standard*, 2 August. https://www.standard.co.uk/business/markets/a-fresh-health-kick-for-fitness-first-boss-andy-cosslett-whos-flexing-his-corporate-muscle-8743387.html (archived at https://perma.cc/TS4R-CNZP)

2 Ashton, J (2019) Leading with James Ashton Episode 2 – Mind and Direct Line, *Apple Podcasts*, 6 May. https://podcasts.apple.com/gb/podcast/episode-2-mind-and-direct-line/id1460796936?i=1000437320566 (archived at https://perma.cc/ZKQ8-BLBG)

3 Ashton, J (2014) To the rescue of Tesco: Dave Lewis's mission to save UK's biggest supermarket, *Evening Standard*, 1 September. https://www.standard.co.uk/lifestyle/london-life/to-the-rescue-of-tesco-dave-lewiss-mission-to-save-the-uk-s-biggest-supermarket-9703451.html (archived at https://perma.cc/UL5V-FERL)

4   Ashton, J (2019) British Council chairman Stevie Spring: 'I like smart power better than soft power', *Telegraph*, 19 December. https://www.telegraph.co.uk/business/2019/12/29/british-council-chairman-stevie-spring-like-smart-power-better/ (archived at https://perma.cc/HZ88-KF4Q)

5   Ashton, J (2019) Leading with James Ashton Episode 2 – Mind and Direct Line, *Apple Podcasts*, 6 May. https://podcasts.apple.com/gb/podcast/episode-2-mind-and-direct-line/id1460796936?i=1000437320566 (archived at https://perma.cc/ZKQ8-BLBG)

6   Ashton, J (2014) BBC Worldwide chief executive Tim Davie: From crisis to drama, the BBC is broadcasting global ambition, *Evening Standard*, 28 March. https://www.standard.co.uk/business/business-news/bbc-worldwide-chief-executive-tim-davie-from-crisis-to-drama-the-bbc-is-broadcasting-global-ambition-9220953.html (archived at https://perma.cc/5YPK-F3BL)

7   Ashton, J (2017) Meet Martina King: The human face of the rise of the machines, *Telegraph*, 20 August. https://www.telegraph.co.uk/business/2017/08/20/meet-martina-king-human-face-rise-machines/ (archived at https://perma.cc/PD3T-8CAG)

8   Ashton, J (2019) Leading with James Ashton Episode 2 – Mind and Direct Line, *Apple Podcasts*, 6 May. https://podcasts.apple.com/gb/podcast/episode-2-mind-and-direct-line/id1460796936?i=1000437320566 (archived at https://perma.cc/ZKQ8-BLBG)

9   Department of Justice (2009) Eli Lilly and Company agrees to pay $1.415 billion to resolve allegations of off-label promotion of Zyprexa [Press Release] https://www.justice.gov/archive/opa/pr/2009/January/09-civ-038.html (archived at https://perma.cc/DTB3-MPX7)

CHAPTER FOUR

Founders

Being the brand

The hubbub in the Virgin Atlantic lounge at London Heathrow was familiar to any frequent flier. Executives hunkered down before boarding their flights to New York or Boston, plugged into hurried phone calls or laser-focused on their laptop screens. Just as many were grazing the buffet, picking from wafer-thin smoked salmon, berries and miniature pastries all washed down with a mid-morning glass of champagne or – for the level-headed – just tea.

To this scene at Heathrow's Terminal 3 one man's arrival introduced a crackle of electricity. Tourists exclaimed to each other and hardened business executives cast too-long glances in the direction of the entrance. The mane of platinum hair, a whiskery grin, darting blue eyes and gentle swagger: Sir Richard Branson, one of the world's best-known business leaders, was instantly recognizable.

As if he was a relative just jetted in from abroad, a swarm of flight attendants and lounge staff gathered round to offer handshakes and kisses. Sir Richard eagerly reciprocated their greetings. A flash of white teeth, a pat on the hand, hugs and waves: the then 64-year-old was in perpetual motion before being ushered into a booth for a quick chat ahead of that day's real performance.

There is something special about Founders. Often they are rich, on occasion they become famous. Usually no one can tell them what to do. They are courted by wealth-obsessed media and feted by governments eager to encourage more start-ups and stay-ups and anyone who can create jobs for their electorate.

Compared with the heady mix of confidence, creative flair and risk taking exuded by Founders, most business leaders pale by their side. The others are the hired help, with contracts that can be torn up at a moment's notice if institutional investors or the board think they have driven down a strategic cul-de-sac and confidence has melted. Founders have earned the right to do as they please. Their easy manner belies years of hard work. The ones that succeed distract from the thousands that didn't.

Those winners were there from the beginning. The empire they sit atop is their baby, their creation, an idea conceived on a crumpled piece of paper or around the kitchen table. It has been brought to life over many years and thanks to many people, all of whom bought into what one woman or man passionately believed would work.

That faith carried them through long nights and moments of self-doubt. It gave them the resolve to turn down generous takeover offers because they knew their vision was bigger than the zeroes on the cheque. It was always about more than just money.

The trouble is that Founders have their limitations too. They are emotional beings. If they want to endure, they must learn how to be great leaders, to transition from swashbuckling entrepreneurship to composed corporate life. The best Founders understand they are not indispensable and there is an obvious time in the best interests of their business to hand over control to someone else. With no one around to say 'No' to them, the worst stick around too long.

Sir Richard Branson is his business. A non-conformist who wore jeans to meetings long before Silicon Valley fashion made dressing down the norm. A disruptor before that meant harnessing the internet to upturn the slow-moving establishment.

Study him up close and he is everything you expect – to a point. He is of course very, very familiar, like a head of state or sporting icon who has been in the public conscious for decades. But with that professional gregariousness of someone who must at all times live his brand, which straddles airlines, mobile phones, banking, hotels and a cruise line, there is also shyness and reserve. This trip for which he had just swept through departures – Virgin Atlantic's inaugural flight to Detroit in summer 2015 – was an ideal opportunity to observe both sides of the billionaire.

Conceived as a marketing exercise by airlines trying to generate some buzz at both ends of a new route, an inaugural flight is essentially a party in the sky. You can imagine that Virgin, which has always accentuated fun to draw attention to itself, is good at them. Over the years, Sir Richard has emerged onto the tarmac from jets in Dubai dressed as Lawrence of Arabia and in Cancun as a Mexican gaucho, always leading the publicity line. For Detroit, a troupe of Motown singers materialized to perform in the aisles at 35,000 feet and Sir Richard executed a mid-air costume change, swapping jacket and crisp white shirt for a black T-shirt that proclaimed 'Detroit Hustles Harder'.

It was a frenetic three days. Perched on a flatbed cradling a mug of tea, Sir Richard granted interviews to all the journalists on board that Virgin had diplomatically herded to premium seats at the front of the plane and plied with fine food and alcohol. He bonded over cocktails with young entrepreneurs who had won the chance to pitch their business idea to him. He talked through the long-winded plan for Heathrow expansion, efforts to get his space venture Virgin Galactic back on track and how he was adjusting to life as a grandparent. He was even happy to oblige when he was pressed on one or two more subjects as he emerged from the loo, even though it was obvious he was ready to switch off the smile.

On landing, Sir Richard joined the mayor of Detroit at a press conference and tried to persuade the city to rehouse homeless Syrians. Then it was off to take questions from a hall full of university students, a bicycle tour around a city still trying to get back on its feet following the decline of the US car industry, another party, and pitching balls at the Detroit Tigers baseball ground. Time was of the essence. Detroit might have been used to hustling, but it was clear who hustled harder.

All the while, Sir Richard had his extrovert streak painted on even though the stunts for which he has gained a reputation don't always sit easily. On another occasion, in Paris in 2006 for the launch of the French offshoot of Virgin Mobile, his challenger phone brand, Sir Richard abseiled down the side of his Virgin Megastore on the Champs Elysees all in black, like a veteran cat burglar. In an unscheduled dash back to London the next day, there was time to talk on the Eurostar. He seemed either nervous or bored, restlessly tearing off small pieces from a newspaper that carried his picture on the front page as question after question was fired at him.

This Founder's leadership secret is to keep things simple. Few can rival him in doing so. Queueing to board the Eurostar train Sir Richard held nothing but a passport, dog-eared and fat with old ticket stubs from criss-crossing the globe. It is the same with his answers which wherever possible do not come with baggage. As the train whizzed through the French countryside, he ranged from green fuels to whether he was going to bid for the next National Lottery licence in the UK. Every time there was a point at which his knowledge dropped off – or the subject was a touchy one – he deferred to a lieutenant somewhere. Most probably it was a clever dodge, or just that this emblem for an empire, co-opted into forever living the brand he created decades ago, has dispensed with details.

Humble and hopeful

The best Founders' stories describe the arc from rags to riches, a favourite newspaper trope. Better still are those prised from the shadows to describe an overnight success that is anything but. Sometimes Founders are ashamed to talk about how it all began. Their aim is always to look forward to the next challenge or opportunity. It is also a long time ago in many cases. They were a different person back then.

Those beginnings are fascinating: that lightbulb moment, the loss of a parent, a redundancy package or simply happenstance. How it began often explains how it continues when they are judged to have made it. It can be corrupting if hunger turns into greed and Founders overreach themselves. Some describe their ongoing drive as originating from a fear of never wanting to be poor again. Leading was never their number one priority.

Ren Zhengfei could not be more different from Sir Richard Branson. An engineer in the People's Liberation Army, he founded Chinese telecoms equipment maker Huawei with a few thousand pounds after he lost his job amid a sweeping round of military cuts. Far from being the promotional frontman, for years he was hidden from view. Huawei expended thousands of dollars touring journalists around its vast campus in Shenzhen, southern China, where information gathering was heavily sanitized. The highlight of these trips, other than the lavish hospitality, was catching a glimpse of the company's own version of the White House, which was perhaps symbolic of the market it most wanted to crack.

Huawei has been hugely successful, building the telecoms networks that are powering the data revolution as well as becoming a big noise in mobile handsets where it slugs it out for market share with Apple and Samsung. As a Chinese company reaching far outside its domestic market, it is a fascinating experiment, although the company's progress in the West is dogged by fears that it is too close to the Chinese government which uses the firm to spy on its customers. The man behind it – who denies all such allegations – works hard to be much less interesting.

The crushing poverty that Ren grew up in prevented him from developing much hinterland. 'Apart from doing the homework I didn't have the opportunity to build a hobby for myself,' he said via an interpreter in 2014, sat in a nondescript room in Westminster crowded with hangers-on. 'I don't even know how to drink and how to smoke. Overall, my personal life is not that colourful.'[1] Nothing to see here, much like the thrifty founder of Swedish furniture chain Ikea, Ingvar Kamprad, who wore second-hand clothes and drove a clapped-out Volvo despite having a £50 billion fortune.

Ren was forced to break for cover when curiosity about Huawei soared. Long before President Trump put the kitmaker on an export blacklist in 2019, which meant it would struggle to buy components from US suppliers, and also leaned on allies not to allow the firm to build out their countries' 5G networks, Ren did his best to distance himself from stories of political influence. He wasn't much of a fan of capitalism either, declaring that 'instinctively I felt that the market economy was about cheating' after he suffered some early setbacks in business building. He added: 'In the army you never talk about money; you only talk about how you can serve the people better.'[2]

Even in 2014, Huawei had upended an industry. It epitomized Chinese corporate power, no matter how homespun the backstory. And it would carry on powering forward. Ren forecast that day that group sales could double to $80 billion in 2018. It sounded fanciful but in the end Huawei surpassed $100 billion over that time-frame. He also pointed out a minor detail about Huawei's copycat White House, remarking that 'the colour is yellow, not white'.

The next challenge

The not-so-rags-to-riches tales of Founders are also impressive, revealing great personal drive beyond merely accruing great wealth. These Founders are the risk takers who were easily bored and not happy with good enough. These are people who have something to lose and stake it on the future anyway.

Lance Uggla was a successful credit trader when he decided to quit Toronto Dominion (TD) Bank to start up on his own in 2003. He was not on the breadline but it did not appear the best time to go it alone. Enron, the energy trader, had collapsed in 2001 and the dotcom bubble was no longer booming. 'I was 39, almost 40, thinking: what's next?' he said in summer 2014 over breakfast in a bustling City of London canteen. 'It really was just a moment in time when you think the risk and reward of something new is worthwhile.'[3]

The challenge for Uggla was that he could not get anywhere on his own. The Canadian-born entrepreneur had spotted a gap in the market. Many of the exotic financial derivatives that had been created over the previous two decades were hard to value. Each investment bank tried its best to track price moves independently. The stubbly and stocky Uggla convinced a dozen institutions to supply him with their data. Based in a barn in St Albans, north of London in the UK, he would aggregate and anonymize this information and sell it back to them.

Given how closely these banks guarded their information, persuading them to pool it with competitors was no easy conversation. Uggla's former employer TD was the first to agree, but only as long as the others came on board. Within a week, they did. In exchange they took an equity stake in Markit, the business Uggla created, which later became IHS Markit through a merger. The institutions still owned a third of Markit when it listed its shares on Nasdaq in 2014. Uggla is a Founder who has kept a tight hold on his business and is profiting handsomely. At the beginning of 2020, he cashed in shares worth $102 million, which left him with a direct residual stake in the business of $188 million.

Early entrepreneurial efforts can occur as part of a process of elimination. Often a start-up comes after a wrong turn when a future Founder realizes they have no desire to work for someone else. Sir Lloyd Dorfman was an investment banker briefly before founding his currency exchange business Travelex from a single outlet in Bloomsbury, central London, in 1976. It went on to trade across the world.

Sometimes the desire comes from a burning ambition to right a wrong or shake up a market. Other times it is trial and error. Guy Hands sold encyclopaedias and then artwork door-to-door long before he learnt his trade at the investment bank Goldman Sachs and then struck it rich as a financier with debt-powered acquisitions of pubs, trains and bookmakers.

What unites many of the most successful Founders is an attention to detail. Former *Daily Express* and *Daily Star* newspaper tycoon Richard Desmond – whose media empire began in 1974 when he co-founded *International Musician and Recording World* – is often pictured puffing cigars in his Thames-side penthouse office. But when his celebrity title *OK!* was launched in 1993 in direct competition with *Hello!*, Desmond drove around supermarkets and newsagents with a pair of scissors to cut open the magazine bundles because retailers weren't putting it on their shelves. 'We thought that more people were interested in Patsy Palmer (Bianca in UK soap opera *EastEnders*) than Princess Schnorbitz of Bratislava,' he said.[4]

Sleepless nights

Founders overlap in some regards with Alphas. Power vests with them; the professional knits seamlessly with the personal. Closer still, a Founder's staff are often family and problems get taken home. It is not always a healthy state of affairs. Debt nearly overwhelmed Surinder Arora's hotels business, making for a more stressful time than he endured building it from nothing.

Arora is not a household name but his story is an eye opener. In 1972, aged 13, he landed at Heathrow Airport in the UK from India without a word of English to be met by a mother he thought was his aunt. After working in

British Airways customer service, handling baggage and later as a financial adviser, he began investing in property.

First of all there was a row of down-at-heel houses opposite Heathrow he offered to overnighting aircrew. In 1999, he opened his first Arora hotel. Now he has a 15-strong portfolio, including Heathrow's Renaissance hotel, where he once waited tables. On a tour around the Continental he opened next to the O2 concert arena along the River Thames in London, it was remarkable to see the affection that staff afforded their leader. Arora knew them all by their first name and many had worked for him elsewhere.

They were foursquare behind his mission: to cater for the concertgoers next door by persuading them an overnight stay would make their trip into London complete. But he also wanted to win business from the West End. Arora wanted to woo the black-tie brigade down from Park Lane to have their celebrations and awards dinners a stone's throw from Greenwich in south east London. You wouldn't bet against him. He has already nabbed the Confederation of British Industry's annual conference, the premium get-together for business leaders and senior politicians that takes place each November. It is a reminder that Founders cast aside caution. They refuse to believe something cannot be done when a typical corporate leader can often be boxed in by convention. And they go fast.

The world's largest hotel groups all granted franchises to Arora when he was a relatively small-scale London hotelier. InterContinental, Accor, Marriott and Hilton: on their behalf he serves passengers coming and going through all of London's major airports.

Such success has taken an almighty charm offensive – and great persistence. But it began with a willingness to change direction. No shrinking wallflower, Arora had been building his hotel empire under the Arora brand, but when Heathrow Airport told him in 2005 that that would not be good enough to get him on the shortlist to operate the new hotel at Terminal 5 (T5), he cast around for a five-star brand he could borrow.

The hotel industry long ago transferred from a property business into one concerned with branding. The big operators sold their freeholds and switched to 'asset-light' models and shovelled cash back to shareholders in the process. But it meant they kept even tighter control over their brands because that was all they had left.

The major players knew Arora well. He could build a property for them at T5, he could even own it, but managing it was a different matter entirely. Unperturbed, Arora narrowed his focus on one firm: Accor. The UK managing director Michael Flaxman was not convinced of the plan but it began to gain traction after an invitation to the group's Paris headquarters. Perhaps the chain's chief executive, Gilles Pélisson, warmed to the Founder spirit he saw. It might even have reminded him of his uncle, Gérard, who set up Accor in 1967.

There were 10 weeks of mystery guest visits to Arora's hotels to assess the experience from all angles. After an arduous process, the entrepreneur won board approval from Paris. Only then did he have to pitch to Heathrow, in competition with every other major hotel group. Three years after being told he didn't stand a chance of operating the new T5 hotel, his 605-bedroom Sofitel opened in 2008.

Six years later, there were sleepless nights when Arora faced a debt squeeze. 'I remember one night being so tearful lying in bed and thinking what had I done to [his wife] Sunita and the kids,' he said.[5] In the end, Davidson Kempner, an American investment manager, took control of two of Arora's hotels after buying a slice of company debt. But rather than being chastened, Arora vowed to learn from the experience. His finances remain conservative in case the global economy nosedives, as it did when the Covid-19 pandemic swept the globe.

With a net worth last recorded at £1.3 billion, Arora hasn't stopped dreaming big. His Western Hub plan proposes to undercut the cost of Heathrow's third runway project, which has been mired for years in political, environmental and economic rows. In February 2020, he even stepped down as chief executive – remaining as chairman – so he had more time to focus on the scheme.

If a Founder lives for their business day and night, when it soars they feel elation and when it crashes they suffer too. Enough time has passed for Chris Anderson to be thoughtful about his own corporate rise and fall. He is best known these days as the man behind the recent growth of TED, once a quirky annual conference of new technology, entertainment and design ideas that has mushroomed into a multimedia empire.

But his first enterprise after newspaper journalism in South Wales in the UK and as a radio producer in the Seychelles was to set up *Future*, a magazine that surfed the wave of the personal computing revolution from 1985 onwards. Anderson's story has some classic rags-to-riches hallmarks: a risky £15,000 loan and starting out using his living room as the office. The business also grew fast and plunged almost as quickly. Future Publishing embraced readers' passions including mountain biking and heavy metal. From a peak stock market valuation of £1.2 billion, the dotcom burst of 2001 got the better of Anderson. Investors who had lauded him at first began to think he was part of the problem.

'I was shaken up,' he said, reflecting in 2017 on those dark days. 'I'd gone from being a business rock star to a total loser in a year, and it really hurt.'[6] In this case it is notable that a Founder hurt by business used business to aid his recovery. Anderson quit Future but took with him one small division, TED, which he described as 'a deeply appealing landing ground'. The asset was injected into his not-for-profit foundation, as if it would be therapeutic to refocus on something so small. The message is clear: going from zero to 90 miles per hour is manageable but the same journey in reverse is too tough for any leader to manage without some form of distraction.

As it turned out, TED was not so much a distraction as a second coming for Anderson. Lightning does not often strike twice to the same extent, but Founders who have set up once have all the skills to do it again – as long as they still have the drive.

Thanks to YouTube, TED has become a phenomenon which in autumn 2012 celebrated the one billionth video view of its TED Talks, the big ideas conveyed by leading academics, statesmen and entrepreneurs in less than 18 minutes while pacing a stage. Recorded in more than 100 languages, they continue to clock up 17 new page views a second.

The American dream

Building the business should be the biggest challenge for any Founder but it is remarkable how starting out and letting go throw up their own challenges. Without resorting to stereotypes, they do these things better in the United States, where confidence overflows and emotions are kept in check where commerce is concerned. Among Silicon Valley Founders, money is as plentiful as ideas, the leadership network is strong, and failure is just fine – as long as it does not last.

In 2008 there was plenty going on in the world to distract from yet another frothy US technology import. A month earlier the UK government had bailed out several banks including the Royal Bank of Scotland, hot on the heels of the collapse of US investment bank Lehman Brothers in September. But Reid Hoffman, the Founder and chairman of LinkedIn, an online network for professionals, denied it was the time to flee from front-line business. A crisis was just the time for Founders to get going.

LinkedIn launched in 2003. It could have been later, but Hoffman couldn't wait to get started again. He promised himself a year off after selling PayPal, his earlier digital payments venture. But in the dotcom collapse of that period he sensed an opportunity and within three months he was back, along with many colleagues from PayPal and his first start-up, an early social networking website called Socialnet.com.

Summing up a Founder's hunger to make a bold idea reality, he said: 'I wanted to create something that would only be possible on the internet, that would get to huge scale, that would change people's lives and become an effective business. I thought: the time is now.'[7]

Sure enough, LinkedIn enjoyed a bumper month for sign-ups when Lehman collapsed and thousands of finance workers found themselves out of a job. Unlike many of its internet peers it was already making a profit. Three years later, the company listed its shares and five years after that Microsoft acquired it for four times the flotation price, a cool $26 billion. Only occasionally do risk-taking Founders get such rich rewards.

Arianna Huffington was also reconciled to moving on. In 2016, her new venture was all about guaranteeing restful nights, something that many Founders do not manage for weeks at a time as they fret about something going wrong in their company.

The Greek-born Huffington is not short of self-belief, having written 15 books, and bestows wisdom easily although she freely admits her accent remains thick enough to give Amazon's Alexa trouble. In the name of plugging her new company Thrive Global, she adopted the unlikely role of shopkeeper, fussing over shelves of rugs, pillows and a vibrating $10,000 sleep pod in an outlet in downtown Manhattan.

The socialite with the bulging contacts book is also an unlikely Founder. *Huffington Post*, the news and views website she launched in 2005, was initially ridiculed as a vanity project but when she sold out to AOL for $315 million six years later the snipers took it more seriously. Founders are usually paid well to part with their life's work and typically incentivized to stay on for three years to ensure the acquisition is bedded down. No longer the boss, few find it hard to exit when the decision to sell has been taken. Having built your own business, taking direction from someone else is not popular.

Walking away five years after the deal was easy for Huffington. She said: 'I will always love the *Huffington Post* but I had zero mixed feelings (about leaving)... If I had stayed, sure I could make incremental improvements and a small difference but I have a great team that I left behind. Here I can build something that can make a real difference to lives around the world.'[8]

Her outlook has much in common with that of Hoffman. Money doesn't come into it – that is often the way for multi-millionaires – but the thrill of the challenge is everything. Founders that have done it once often start up again following a similar pattern. Thrive, a venture designed to help companies and individuals boost their well-being, united many of the same staff and same investors in the very same office space where HuffPo was brought to life.

Letting go

In 1981 seven colleagues quit Patni Computer Systems in Pune, India to set up on their own. From a small flat with just $250 of funds they created Infosys, which became a pioneer of the new IT revolution. For the first time, US and European blue-chip companies could strip cost from their business by outsourcing software and systems work to experts in lower-cost India.

These seven Founders were reluctant to let go through economic ups and downs and when Infosys was squeezed between faster-moving domestic rivals and IBM and Accenture abroad. Remarkably, it wasn't until 2014 that someone other than a Founder was appointed to lead the company.

Interviewed a year before that, one of the Founders, Kris Gopalakrishnan, confessed his reluctance to look outside. 'If we have a sufficient number of leaders internally – and it is our job to create those leaders – then hopefully they will select somebody from inside,' he said.[9]

The 2014 appointment did not go well. Hired from the German software group SAP, Vishal Sikka lasted only three years, citing 'personal attacks' when he stepped down. Despite allegations that had been repeatedly proven false and baseless by independent investigations, 'the attacks continue, and worse still, amplified by the very people from whom we all expected the most steadfast support in this great transformation,' he wrote in his resignation email to the board in August 2017.[10]

Without publicly criticizing Sikka, another Founder, Narayana Murthy, wrote to the board with the plea: 'We just do not want the board to drive this institution to death through serious governance deficits in our own lifetime.'[11] The Infosys board retorted that Murthy's campaign 'has had the unfortunate effect to undermine the company's efforts to transform itself'[12] and largely blamed him for Sikka's exit. What a mess. If the firm had been disentangled from its Founders earlier, the process might not have been so traumatic.

After 17 years in charge, Lance Uggla at IHS Markit is a rarity. In a 2008 *Harvard Business Review* article, Professor Noam Wasserman found in a study of 212 US start-ups from the late 1990s and early 2000s that by the time ventures reached their third birthday, 50 per cent of founders were no longer chief executive. In year four that fell to 40 per cent, and fewer than 25 per cent led their companies' initial public offering.[13]

It can be a tortured decision to take. Peter Cruddas founded the British City spread-betting firm CMC Markets with £10,000 in 1989, but struggled with letting anyone else run the company for him. For several years he acted as chairman, having handed day-to-day control to a chief executive. But that left him in a bind, because he felt he had to back the boss even when he saw things going on that he didn't agree with. Cruddas reinstated himself in 2013 after resigning from the Conservative party, where he had been co-treasurer, and committed himself to run CMC for a decade. 'I am less stressed now by being the chief executive because I can change things,' he said in 2014.[14]

Tall and imperious, Cruddas believes that no Founder can afford to have an off switch. His phone stays close if he is lying on a sun lounger. He reasons that when you have your own company it is ridiculous to think you can detach yourself for as a long as a fortnight.

Soon after his reinstatement, a new challenge emerged. Cruddas successfully floated the company on the London Stock Exchange in 2016, crystallizing huge fortunes for many of his loyal staff. But corporate governance rules meant he could no longer be omnipotent – CMC had to appoint a chairman to run the board when he had spent so many years ruling the roost. Applying these human checks and balances is the price of admission to the public markets. Investors don't mind autocrats – there are plenty that have emerged from Silicon Valley and they are discussed in the Alphas chapter. But external shareholders require that they are kept in the loop and performance remains strong. Most Founders have a straight choice to make between wealth or absolute power.

In 1999, Jo Malone judged she had taken her eponymous fragrance line as far as she could, selling out to the Estée Lauder beauty empire. The control she sacrificed was over her name. When she re-entered the market many years later it was under the banner of Jo Loves.

Strong foundations

And so back to Sir Richard Branson. How it all began has passed into folklore, not least because the Virgin entrepreneur has written seven books chronicling his life and times and lessons on entrepreneurship. Born to well-to-do Surrey parents, he discovered a moneymaking bent while still at prep school. His first scheme, to breed and sell budgerigars, was a failure. Sir Richard quit education to concentrate on *Student*, the magazine he set up, with his headteacher's prognosis ringing in his ears: he would either end up in prison or become a millionaire. The magazine morphed into a mail-order business and then a record shop. It was christened Virgin because his team were all complete virgins at business.

Keen to challenge the norm, Sir Richard's efforts to upturn the establishment – in the same way he used to flip air hostesses into the air for a joke – cantered through the music industry, aviation and trains. He surrounded himself with much drier figures, long-serving lieutenants who counted the takings and cut the deals while he flitted around, sprinkling fairy dust, exciting the consumer and tweaking the tail of the competition.

For 50 years he has preserved a marvellous elixir, creating 18 billion-dollar companies and organizations from scratch in 12 different sectors. Virgin is the best challenger brand in the world, deployed in numerous territories and industries. In the US and Australia, there have been short-haul airlines. In the UK, the brand was assumed by NTL and Telewest, the two cable TV challengers to Rupert Murdoch's pay-TV platform BSkyB, in 2006. The merged cable firms acquired Virgin Mobile with the express purpose of running the entire business under the Virgin banner.

Twelve years later in 2018, CYBG, home of the decades-old Clydesdale and Yorkshire banking brands, did precisely the same thing. It paid £1.7 billion for Virgin Money, a venture founded on assets of the collapsed Northern Rock. Bosses believed that the enlarged firm, using the Virgin moniker, had a better chance of wrestling customers from the establishment UK lenders of HSBC, Lloyds, Barclays and NatWest.

Meanwhile, arguably the world's most famous Founder has seen his role morph into that of marketer-in-chief, which is precisely what was on display over those several days in Detroit in 2015. Even so, his appearances and communication are carefully metered. Many of the companies that take the Virgin name get only a sliver of Sir Richard's time for promotional purposes.

What is clear is that although the Founder and his family still own the business, Sir Richard's day-to-day involvement is limited. But there was no parting of the ways, no going on for too long. Any angst over handing over the reins was long ago and kept in the background.

Since 2011 the Virgin empire has been run by a clean-cut lawyer from New Zealand. It wouldn't do to describe Josh Bayliss as the brains of Virgin while Sir Richard remains its heart and soul, but the Kiwi has been determined to professionalize the group – and that means thinking about life when the Founder is no longer around to lead promotions.

Bayliss is not the first. Before him, there was Stephen Murphy, a former Mars and Unilever accountant who was chief executive for six years, having joined Virgin in 1994 to restructure the business after the sale of Virgin Music.

Virgin looks different over the last decade. There has been a concerted effort to shift its business model from taking a share of the profits to raking in royalties from its all-powerful brand. Virgin can recycle its capital into new ventures by selling down its shares in gyms and banks where other investors are prepared to stump up equity. Those companies that take the brand hand over a slice of revenues for the privilege of using the name.

It gives Sir Richard the best of both worlds. The image of the fun-loving corporate disruptor lingers but in reality he concentrates on charitable endeavours through his nonprofit foundation Virgin Unite, or specific new ventures such as blasting off into space with Virgin Galactic. There have been missteps – such as seeking financial support for Virgin Atlantic from the UK government during the Covid-19 outbreak – but the brand has maintained its youthful vigour even though its Founder turned 70 in July 2020. It is doubtful that this model could work for any other enterprise.

Every other Founder must stick or twist: decide when their venture is better off without them. But even hands-off, Sir Richard is the business.

'This is a family business but I'm not one of the family,' Josh Bayliss said in 2016. 'I go to Necker Island for board meetings, not for kitesurfing.'[15] Bayliss is crucial because it is unclear whether either of Sir Richard's children, Sam and Holly, who have kept busy with film-making and philanthropy, will ever want to take over the reins at Virgin. Their father may have shown them the route that means they don't have to.

The siblings are part of Virgin management, with Holly, who began as an intern in 2008, seemingly more deeply involved in group activities, chairing Virgin Unite. The choices ahead for them are familiar for any Scion, as explored in the next chapter.

FOUNDERS IN BRIEF

Strengths: Courage, drive, passion, non-conformity.

Weaknesses: Lack of self-awareness, emotional, unable to switch off.

Suitability: Founding companies.

Where you will find them: At the helm of something they set up. No one else would employ them.

Endnotes

1   Ashton, J (2014) Huawei founder brushes off accusations that it acts as an arm of the Chinese state, *Independent*, 2 May. https://www. independent.co.uk/news/business/analysis-and-features/huawei-founder-brushes-off-accusations-that-it-acts-as-an-arm-of-the-chinese-state-9319244.html (archived at https://perma.cc/L2H5-G8MM)

2 Ibid.

3 Ashton, J (2014) Interview: Markit chief Lance Uggla – 'How I crunched the numbers to create a £500m City fortune', *Evening Standard*, 27 June. https://www.standard.co.uk/business/markets/interview-markit-chief-lance-uggla-how-i-crunched-the-numbers-to-create-a-500m-city-fortune-9567555.html (archived at https://perma.cc/R5R4-RGUD)

4 Ashton, J (2010) All cash and no prey for Desmond, *The Times*, 18 April. https://www.thetimes.co.uk/article/all-cash-and-no-prey-for-desmond-vtdxjtk3rgg (archived at https://perma.cc/94BM-ULGH)

5 Ashton, J (2016) Heathrow hotelier has his sights on the sky but feet firmly on the ground, *The Times*, 19 August. https://www.thetimes.co.uk/article/heathrow-hotelier-has-his-sights-on-the-sky-but-feet-firmly-on-the-ground-7kfld9q75 (archived at https://perma.cc/8JND-Z4XC)

6 Ashton, J (2017) TED Talks owner Chris Anderson on the power of public speaking and being the ultimate influencer, *Evening Standard*, 1 March. https://www.standard.co.uk/lifestyle/london-life/ted-talks-owner-chris-anderson-on-the-power-of-public-speaking-and-being-the-ultimate-influencer-a3478766.html (archived at https://perma.cc/6HFF-898F)

7 Ashton, J (2008) Networker seizes the day, *Sunday Times*, 30 November

8 Ashton, J (2016) Arianna Huffington on why we should all be sleeping our way to the top, *Evening Standard*, 14 December. https://www.standard.co.uk/lifestyle/london-life/arianna-huffington-on-why-we-should-all-be-sleeping-our-way-to-the-top-a3419831.html (archived at https://perma.cc/YTQ9-KFX8)

9 Ashton, J (2013) It's all systems go for Kris Gopalakrishnan, the IT chief rebooting India's economic dream, *Evening Standard*, 28 June. https://www.standard.co.uk/business/markets/it-s-all-systems-go-for-kris-gopalakrishnan-the-it-chief-rebooting-india-s-economic-dream-8678200.html (archived at https://perma.cc/SSA4-T6XQ)

10 Infosys (2017) Annexure A: Resignation email received from the Vishal Sikka, MD and CEO by the board of directors, Press Release, 18 August. https://www.infosys.com/newsroom/press-releases/documents/2017/annexure-a-company-statement-18aug2017.pdf (archived at https://perma.cc/YA34-LS66)

11 First Post Staff (2017) Infosys Vishal Sikka resigns: Text of NR Narayana Murthy's letter to set 'record straight', *First Post*, 19 August. https://www.firstpost.com/business/infosys-vishal-sikka-resigns-text-of-nr-narayana-murthys-letter-to-set-record-straight-3946501.html (archived at https://perma.cc/GA2B-C2RV)

12 Infosys (2017) Company Statement, Press Release, 18 August. https://www.infosys.com/newsroom/press-releases/2017/company-statement-18august2017.html (archived at https://perma.cc/39UE-D9YQ)

13 Wasserman, N (2008) The Founder's dilemma, *Harvard Business Review*, February. https://hbr.org/2008/02/the-founders-dilemma (archived at https://perma.cc/9QGH-CDTX)

14 Ashton, J (2014) Interview: Peter Cruddas, CMC Markets – Dressed for success, spread-betting tycoon who's walking tall once more, *Evening Standard*, 31 October. https://www.standard.co.uk/business/markets/interview-peter-cruddas-cmc-markets-dressed-for-success-spread-betting-tycoon-who-s-walking-tall-9830820.html (archived at https://perma.cc/8NHT-A4YH)

15 Ashton, J (2016) The man who is leading Virgin into space, the US – and NHS... and no, we don't mean Sir Richard Branson, *Mail on Sunday*, 30 July. https://www.thisismoney.co.uk/money/markets/article-3716186/The-man-leading-Virgin-space-NHS-no-don-t-mean-Sir-Richard-Branson.html (archived at https://perma.cc/J2Q8-77F9)

CHAPTER FIVE

Scions

Prove yourself

Standing in one of Deutsche Telekom's yellow phone boxes in Hamburg's city centre, Jean-François Decaux had his father's words ringing in his ears. It was September 1982 and this was his family firm's first incursion into the German market. Back home in France, JCDecaux's bus shelters had become a familiar sight in many towns and cities, installed and maintained in return for the company earning a fee from the advertising panels they incorporated.

But in Germany, there was nothing: no advertising inventory, no office, not even a telephone line – which was why Decaux began making calls to drum up trade from the street.

What he did have was a challenge from his father Jean-Claude, who had set up the company that bore their names 18 years earlier and had already expanded beyond its home market into Belgium and Portugal. There is no job for you with me in France, the law graduate had been told. If you want to join the family firm, pick your own market and grow it from scratch.

Decaux junior chose Germany because he had studied the German language at school. What he didn't realize was that 60 per cent of the market was controlled by a company owned by the local authorities of Frankfurt and Munich among others, which meant his biggest potential customers were also invested in his greatest rival. Yet if he wanted to get on, he knew that failure was not an option.

'My father said to me, "I'm going to bet five million Deutschmarks on you,"' Decaux recalled. 'He said, "I don't speak German; I don't want to go there. You go there, you know how the business model works because you grew up in the middle of this. If you lose the money, you will still be my son, but you will not be fit for this business."'

Now the smooth and confident co-chief executive of JCDecaux, it is clear the bet paid off. As of the end of 2019, the company employed more than 13,000 staff and operated more than 1 million advertising panels, counting a daily audience of over 890 million people. JCDecaux reported net income of €266 million on revenues of €3.9 billion, having expanded from bus shelters to all forms of out-of-home advertising – billboards, airports, city cycling schemes and public toilets. Today its kiosks and litter bins stud the pedestrianized heart of many of the world's largest cities, and its digital poster hoardings line busy thoroughfares.

Decaux added: 'I could easily have gone to work for L'Oréal or Procter & Gamble but proving to my father that I was capable of meeting the challenge was something which was very appealing for me.'

Decaux is a Scion, a leader that assumed control of their family firm. Scions' leadership opportunities arise because their father, grandfather or another antecedent built a business before them. They are the chosen ones, growing up knowing that one day all this will be theirs. But with a comfortable childhood and the trappings of wealth comes the knowledge that the pressure of living up to your name lies ahead.

It is a leadership type that is fraught with challenges. Scions often follow in the footsteps of Founders who worry that their children are not hungry for success as they were. Some embrace their family empire and succeed in growing and improving it, by learning from their parent but modernizing when necessary and perhaps surrounding themselves with cleverer lieutenants. Some divert from the legacy, moving quickly to take the enterprise off in a whole new direction – and not always yielding the best results.

Some sons and daughters of great leaders relax into the roles they inherit – or redefine them into something they are more comfortable with. They must be careful. It takes a handful of generations to build an empire, but sometimes only one to sweep it away. And the tough decisions required by Scions can be coloured by preserving the broader family's primary source of income and oftentimes navigating sibling rivalry.

Betting on the bloodline

Jean-Claude Decaux was eager for his sons to be as hungry as he had been. Born into a family of modest means in Beauvais, north of Paris, in 1937, he showed early entrepreneurial flair by putting up posters around town to promote his parents' shoe shop. Left in charge for a whole summer, sales went through the roof despite the town having emptied out. However, his father returned from vacation to complaints that some of the advertisements were displayed illegally and a row ensued.

'My grandmother was much more commercially minded and said, "Look at the sales, look at the bottom line. Jean-Claude did an amazing job,"' Decaux said. Because he was not yet 21, Jean-Claude needed his father's signature to open a bank account and start his own bill poster business. When the French government imposed punitive taxes on roadside advertising, he was forced to think again and in 1964 came up with the idea of bus shelters, which he offered to install for municipalities all over France in exchange for selling advertising on the side of them. 'I never envisaged working for anyone other than myself,' he once said, 'because I had an impossible temperament!'[1]

The Decaux creative spirit was found to be alive and well in his eldest son. Jean-François managed to convince the mayor of Hamburg, Germany's second-largest city and one of the few not involved with the state-run competitor, to enter into a 20-year contract for providing the so-called 'street furniture' his father had patented. More followed. The family's competitive streak paid dividends, he said, but its name – which had growing renown in France, but was unknown in Germany – did not. There was also some luck, he conceded. 'The market leader was not reacting very quickly. I think in today's world, I wouldn't have been able to succeed as much because the company would have probably copied our model very quickly. We had almost no competition for two years.'

Fast forward to October 1989 and Decaux was still outpacing his rivals – and no longer making calls from the street. The week after the Berlin Wall fell, he was pitching his services to Leipzig and Dresden among other East German cities so that Decaux was operating there even before German reunification had taken place. Pleased with the results, it was no surprise that his father sanctioned sending his two other sons, Jean-Charles and Jean-Sébastien, to develop Spain and Italy respectively when they joined the family firm in 1989 and 1998.

Moving to London, Jean-François took on more responsibility, expanding in the UK and the Nordics and then to the US, Russia and beyond. Scions learn from their parent and then eventually take over from them. At JCDecaux, the balance of power was shifting towards the end of the century when Jean-Claude, Jean-François and Jean-Charles – who had focused his efforts on Southern Europe, Latin American and Asia – were invited to lunch in New York with the leader of CBS, Mel Karmazin.

It was a case of strength in numbers. The US group was best known for its network television station but as the media industry consolidated it had already gained exposure to outdoor advertising because its radio network Infinity had acquired the transport panels firm TDI in

May 1996. The Decaux trio suspected CBS was in the market for further deals. Sure enough, they were made a generous offer for their company over lunch.

'We politely said we were going to think about it,' Decaux said. 'And in the lift going down my father said to me, "It's your decision, it's your story now. But if you accept that you will have a lot of money, you're going to be bored, you're going to divorce, you're going to lose a lot of money and you will end up investing in things about which you have no clue." In less than five minutes after the lunch we decided not to sell, to take on the American guys and go public.'

Jean-Claude had been very much against mergers and acquisitions. The business he built was forged by striking contract after contract with cities around the world. Encouraged by his sons, that changed in 1998 when Clear Channel, another US rival, beat JCDecaux to acquire the London-based More Group, which had a presence in 25 countries. The Scions persuaded their father that because their industry was scaling up fast, they either had to become an acquiring company or simply sell out.

In April 1999, some months after the CBS lunch, JCDecaux doubled in size with the £650 million acquisition of Avenir, the outdoor arm of French advertising group Havas. A month later, CBS paid $6.5 billion in stock to buy Outdoor Systems, the largest US billboard company. It was game on. To pay down the debt taken on through the deal, JCDecaux listed on the Paris Euronext exchange in 2001.

The handover

By this time, the company leadership that largely endures to this day had been established: Jean-François and Jean-Charles as co-chief executives, with the chairman's role passing between them every year. As chair of the supervisory board, Jean-Claude was by now detached from the day-to-day running of the business. Even his idea for succession was robustly debated and ultimately rejected. The Founder suggested his eldest son Jean-François should become chief executive, handing over to Jean-Charles when he reached the age of 60. Jean-François said he wanted to share the role with his brother, because each knew several major markets extremely well and they could complement each other. So much for sibling rivalry, which can rip steady family firms apart.

'This probably cemented our relationship even further, because I think a lot of sons would have said, "Okay, I'll take the CEO position, you are on the waiting list,"' said Decaux. 'I didn't do that and I think that proved to my brother I respected him and valued immensely what he added to the business.'

The Scion can think of only one notable disagreement with his father, which in 1992 centred around entering the US market. Jean-Claude was good friends with Marcel Bich, co-founder of the Bic ballpoint pen company which also made cigarette lighters and other disposable items. Problems with exploding lighters had led to a rash of US class actions and Decaux did not want to face the same if his automated public toilets were to malfunction.

'He told me, "I know it's the biggest market in the world but I don't want to risk the company that I built from scratch just for you to win San Francisco and a few American cities."' In the end, Jean-François pushed ahead, emboldened by the unlikely support of the film director Francis Ford Coppola, who appeared at a public hearing on the matter to sing the loos' praises after spotting them while filming in Europe.

By respecting tradition, establishing clear responsibilities and conducting some robust debates, JCDecaux has demonstrated how handing over to not one but two Scions can work effectively. The Founder was willing to cede leadership, the Scions were tested early and hungry for the challenge. Now plans are in train to involve the third generation of the family.

Banking on succession

At 7.47 am on 10 September 2014, Banco Santander disclosed to the world that its powerful leader had died.

Emilio Botín was a giant of the banking world. Known as 'El Presidente' to his staff, over almost 30 years he turned a little-known Spanish lender named after an unremarkable northern port city into a global brand, snapping up banks in the UK, US and Latin America. Becoming chairman in 1986, the same year that Spain joined the European Community, Botín understood the opportunities that being part of a larger trading bloc would bring. By the time of his death, Santander was the largest bank in the eurozone by market capitalization, managing funds worth

€.24 trillion on behalf of 103 million customers, maintaining nearly 14,000 bank branches and employing over 182,000 staff.

At 4.44 pm on the same September day, a statement was issued by Santander. While expressing 'deep sorrow' at the loss of Botín, the board of directors announced that, following a meeting of the appointments and remuneration committee that morning, they had unanimously agreed to appoint his daughter, Ana Botín, as Santander's new chair. The committee considered the 53-year-old to be 'the most appropriate person, given her personal and professional qualities, experience, track record in the Group and her unanimous recognition both in Spain and internationally'.[2]

Ana Botín's response ran: 'In these difficult times for me and my family, I appreciate the trust of the board of directors and I am fully committed to my new responsibilities. I have been working at Grupo Santander in different countries and with different responsibilities for many years and I have experienced the professionalism and dedication of our teams. We'll continue to dedicate all our efforts with total determination to keep building a better bank for our customers, employees and shareholders.'

What a remarkable 24 hours it had been. It was only on the Tuesday evening that Emilio Botín had passed away after suffering a heart attack. His daughter, the eldest of six children, flew to Madrid from the UK early on Wednesday morning and before the end of the working day she had been elevated in his place. At a moment when time stands still for most families as they unite to grieve, commemorate and reflect on the loss of a loved one, corporate life did not just carry on but appears to have sped up. While the Botín clan is certain to have gone through the same sad process that every stricken family goes through, the business world abhors a vacuum.

The alacrity with which Santander chose its new chairman was helped by the fact that the appointment of Ana Botín was all but a forgone conclusion. Despite the air of due process, it was written in the stars that she would one day succeed her father as he had succeeded his father and so on. The roots that entwine the business and the family go back further. Banco de Santander was created in 1857. A Botín was managing director of the institution as early as 1895 and Ana's grandfather became permanent chairman in 1923.[3]

They are talked of as European banking royalty, so it was no surprise that this appointment – for its speed and predictability – looked more like a coronation than a rigorous corporate succession. And all this despite the Botín family owning barely a 2 per cent stake in the business. No wonder some of Santander's shareholders grumbled that they were not properly consulted. It backed up the saying inside the bank: 'En Santander, o eres Botínes o eres botones.' ('At Santander, if you're not a Botín, then you're just a bellhop.')

Scions know that family means business. That they will one day lead is a calling sometimes drummed into them from an early age. Emilio Botín hadn't always put his family first, however. Ana Botín had been fired by her father only 15 years earlier. In 1999 she was already scaling the organization but to ensure smooth passage of the takeover of Banco Central Hispano (BCH), which was to make Santander Spain's number one lender, Emilio asked her to leave to assuage the concerns of revolting BCH executives that she was already being groomed for the top.

'To me it proves that he always thought first about what was good for Santander rather than about himself and his family or other personal issues,' she said in a 2015 interview.[4] In the same conversation, she played down the idea of the dynasty being extended when she steps down, saying, 'The chances of that happening would be very small.'

For all the supposed lack of sentimentality, Ana Botín – who is incredibly sharp, witty, brusque – was not long in the wilderness. After three years in which she ran a small venture capital firm and consultancy she was asked back to lead the group's Banesto subsidiary in Madrid. A bigger test came in 2010 when she took over at the helm of Santander UK, a scale player in savings and mortgages stitched together from three smaller lenders: Abbey, Alliance & Leicester and Bradford & Bingley.

In 2013, when asked about the best advice she had received in her career, Botín did not stray far from home. 'It is going to sound clichéd but my husband has been incredibly helpful,' she said. 'I never speak a lot about women's things but you can't have a family and a professional life if you don't work as a team. For me, my husband gives me advice all the time – he's been very supportive.'[5]

Like a number of Scions, Botín had worked for many years in the shadow of her father. Emilio was a classic Alpha leader, conversing with presidents and royalty, leading with an iron grip and creator of a corporate palace of his own. He oversaw the construction of Santander Group

City, a grand headquarters built in the Boadilla del Monte district of Madrid, which opened in 2004. At 250 hectares it houses nine office buildings, a residential training facility, Europe's largest corporate nursery with a capacity for up to 500 children and extensive sports facilities including two golf courses on which Botín could frequently be found at lunchtime.

But when she finally got the top job, Ana Botín proved she was not afraid of tinkering with her father's legacy. Out went several key lieutenants, the breakneck deal making and generous shareholder rewards. In came more prudent finances including a dividend cut and balance sheet repair, as shown by the €7.5 billion fundraising launched just four months after she took the helm. Botín emphasized a focus on organic growth, such as how to drive more revenue from the bank's customer base by forging closer relationships and cross-selling products, as well as targeting some mundane but essential areas of corporate lending like supply chain finance.

It wasn't quite simplicity first, but a line was drawn under complexity. For example, the habit of locally listing shares in many of Santander's country operations went out of vogue. But Ana Botín had little choice. The bank had to change because times had changed. Even without her father's death, the bank was due fresh blood and a new direction. The question is whether a Scion was the best person to shake up Santander. A Fixer would have done more and faster, unburdened with legacy.

Even before the impact of Covid-19 had taken its toll, by the start of 2020 Santander shares had more than halved on Ana Botín's watch. Ultra-low interest rates made it hard to make money and European banking shares have been out of favour for several years. Some Scions succeed in eclipsing their parent. On the strength of Ana's first five years, that achievement appears some way off at Santander.

The glint of ambition

One entrepreneur that has eclipsed his father is steel magnate Lakshmi Mittal, whose ArcelorMittal empire recorded revenues in excess of $70 billion in 2019, although lower steel prices drove the group to a bumper $2.5 billion net loss. Mittal, named after the Hindu goddess of wealth, started out in his father's steel firm, joining at the age of 19, although life was nearly very different. Born in the desert north of India to a home with no electricity, he was sent by his father to study at St Xavier's College in Kolkata. His principal wanted him to be a professor.

Mittal's first career test came in his mid-twenties, setting up a plant in Indonesia that his father had not been sure about. Eventually the family firm was split in 1995 – amid reports of some tension – so that the Scion could develop the international arm and his father Mohan Lal Mittal and brothers could concentrate on the Indian assets.

Mittal's empire today encompasses 191,000 employees and manufactures steel in 18 countries.

What is clear is that Mittal – who in person is not steely, but contemplative and almost shy – has grown his business with family in mind. Just as he was granted early opportunities, he made sure his offspring have had similar chances. Mittal's son Aditya has worked alongside him for many years. This Scion has formed much more of a double act than some father–son leadership combinations. Aditya's sister Vanisha has also sat on the board as a non-executive director since 2004.

Despite this idea that Scions are somehow mollycoddled within the family firm – that taking up a job with their parent is the easy option rather than striking out on their own – once again here is an example of a Scion who has been piled up with responsibility early on, not protected from it. As the finance director of Mittal Steel, at the age of 30 Aditya played a key role in the 2006 merger with Arcelor of Luxembourg that created an industrial giant, the first firm in the world to produce 100 million tonnes of steel in a year.

In a 2012 interview Mittal senior emphasized that his son could go his own way just as he had – at the same time predicting that he would not leave ArcelorMittal. 'First of all I don't think he would like to do it but everyone should be given freedom to do whatever they want,' he said. 'My father did not hold me; I cannot hold my son or daughter. But I believe he will stay: as far as I know today, he would like to continue to grow with the organization.'[6]

So far he has been proved right. On top of his finance role and leading the group's European operations, Aditya was also appointed president in 2018, with Mittal senior declaring, 'He will continue to work with me in shaping the future strategic direction of the group.'[7] And when in 2020 ArcelorMittal bought Essar Steel in India, Aditya was made chairman of the renamed venture with an ambition to ramp up supply.

These appointments were not overnight decisions taken by Mittal senior. Scions understand the benefit of long-term thinking. The fact that they have been put in charge suggests there has been sufficient success to hand something on to the next generation. Trust has endured. There has been no reason to stray from the path, no need for a shake-up by parachuting in another leadership type such as a Seller, Lover or Fixer to mend a troubled situation or a Diplomat to mediate.

The dividends that longevity brings are something the Wallenbergs of Sweden have understood for generations. Their dynasty is one of the most powerful business families in Europe. Through the holding company Investor, the fifth generation of Wallenbergs manage an empire that includes significant stakes in many of the country's biggest companies including appliance firm Electrolux, telecoms equipment maker Ericsson, pharmaceuticals giant Astra-Zeneca and in banking, SEB, as well as US exchange group Nasdaq and the private equity investor EQT. Investor's portfolio was valued at 485 billion Swedish kroner (£41 billion) at the end of 2019.

These are different types of Scions, running an investment portfolio for the long term, rather than occupying the operational roles described elsewhere in this chapter. Yet Jacob Wallenberg, chairman since 2005, is thoughtful about how the family acts today and conscious of how the levers of influence have changed over the years.

'When my grandfather walked into a boardroom, regardless whether he owned a single share or not, he would command the day,' he said in one interview.[8] 'His power was based on the strength of his personality and his position in society. When his son – my father – walked into the same boardroom 25 years later, it was not enough to be a strong and well-respected individual. He had to carry some weight in terms of ownership – let's say 10 per cent of the company – in order to be considered the leading voice at the table. When today's generation walks into the same boardroom, it is only ownership that counts and not a name, however great and renowned it might be.'

Like Ana Botín, Jacob Wallenberg spent time away before joining and gradually moving up through the family firm. After graduating from Wharton Business School he spent two years on Wall Street with investment bank JP Morgan before a stint in London with Hambros, the merchant bank, and then journeying to Asia with SEB. That meant he developed a valuable international outlook that is common in a small market like Sweden, but not easily picked up by spending all of your formative years working in the capital Stockholm.

Now he is the leader, he talks as if he must overcompensate for the name he carries so as not to appear a relic in the boardroom incapable of offering leadership. Investor's network of analysts is there to ensure that its directors remain incredibly well informed about their investee companies and the markets they operate in. For the Wallenbergs, it is ownership plus knowledge that legitimize the leadership they offer, not their name. Wallenberg added, 'Our purpose is to be recognized as very professional and knowledgeable board members. The other board members not only respect this, they also listen to us. Only by making our voice heard will we make an impact on a company.'[9]

He described as 'dynamic continuity' the process of always changing to keep up with a changing world, within the framework of Investor's clear business model. 'But does that have anything to do with being a family business? No, it has to do with the values that our ancestors formulated and that we have tested and continue to respect.' The message is that being a Scion gets you a foot in the door, but is no guarantee of effectiveness.

And yet for all the professionalism and training that go into living up to their family title, some Scions cannot fail to betray their emotions. Yes, it's business, but for them it is so much more than that.

Lord (Jonathan) Rothermere assumed the chairmanship of Daily Mail and General Trust (DMGT) on his father's death in 1998. The group was listed on the London Stock Exchange in 1932, a decade after it was established to manage the Harmsworth family's interests that had expanded since brothers Alfred and Harold – Jonathan's great-grandfather – began publishing the *Daily Mail* in 1896. Over the years, the firm has diversified into trade conferences, websites and information companies and has been large enough to move in and out of the FTSE 100.

The flagship *Daily Mail* has grown in influence as the voice of Middle England with enough bite to keep British government ministers awake at night. But the challenging economics of newspapers has led to some tough decisions. In 2009, DMGT announced it was selling control of the loss-making *London Evening Standard* to the former KGB agent Alexander Lebedev for a token £1. The *Standard* remained a fixture on street corners all over the capital but it was bought by a dwindling band of commuters as their essential home-time read.

For Rothermere, the group's chairman and controlling shareholder, the disposal was obviously a tough decision. 'I am very emotionally attached to the *Standard*,' he said soon after the sale was made public. 'Along with the death of my parents, [selling] it has been one of the hardest things to live through in my life.'[10] Day-to-day decision making is left to DMGT's chief executive but in Rothermere's mind, the two things, family and business, are inextricably linked. His father had acquired the *Standard* in 1987.

As the Lovers demonstrate in the next chapter, passion in leadership should be welcomed, as long as it does not make for emotive decision making. DMGT might no longer be one of the UK's leading newspaper publishers if a Scion with ink in his veins did not control it. So many other print companies long ago got out of the dead trees business in pursuit of faster growth away from consumer media.

It is a fair bet that Rothermere will never do that, judging that a conglomerate structure will comprise assets that are intended to offset the decline of newspapers. Scions succeed if they surround themselves with able lieutenants – as long as they take on board their recommended course of action from time to time. The next generation has a long time to listen and learn. Rothermere's eldest son, Vere, joined DMGT in a business development role at the start of 2020, according to his LinkedIn account.[11]

Managing risk

When Jean-Claude Decaux finally retired, it was not without ensuring his family remained tightly entwined with the outdoor advertising business he had founded. At a supervisory board meeting on 8 April 2013, he announced he would not seek renewal of his board membership past the annual shareholders' meeting on 15 May that year. The family still owned 66 per cent of the company, which by this point was worth more than €4 billion, but Decaux was leaving nothing to chance. Expressing his wish to see the involvement of a third generation in the firm, one of three appointees to the supervisory board just as he was leaving was Alexia Decaux-Lefort, his eldest granddaughter, who is a product manager at Piaget, the luxury Swiss watchmaker. Until his death in 2016, Jean-Claude held the title of founder and honorary chairman.

The door is open to the next generation to take an active involvement in JCDecaux, according to Jean-François Decaux, but the kind of challenge he was thrown in 1982 is not there anymore at a company that operates in more than 80 countries from Australia to Zimbabwe. 'It's a different story for them,' he said. 'You need to have another experience elsewhere for 10 years. Then, if you prove yourself in some other business, you can join the family company.'

In 2017 the three brothers made a decision on behalf of G3, as their children are collectively known internally. The Decaux family invested €791 million to take a stake in Eurazeo, an investment house created by the merchant bank Lazard and its founders. The family business awaits the next set of Decaux Scions, but their investments are already diversified away from the media industry – just in case G3 does not emulate the success of G2.

The issue of diversification weighs heavily on Scions. Businesses cannot be preserved in aspic. Only leaders can decide how best to combine the traditions of the past with sound strategic moves that will guarantee a future. What haunts them is that it will all crumble on their watch, fulfilling the proverbial 'from shirtsleeves to shirtsleeves in three generations'.

Trading up

Some are subtle and successful such as the transformation of Pinault-Printemps-Redoute (PPR) into Kering. In a 2014 article, François-Henri Pinault, chairman and chief executive of the French luxury goods house, described the handover of power from his father François, who founded the company in 1963.[12]

There was clarity in the process. After a dinner in Paris one Thursday night in 2003 at which father asked son to take over running the family holding company Artemis, François-Henri arrived at the headquarters the following Monday to find the furniture had been switched over the weekend so that now he inhabited the corner office.

Two years later when he also took over leadership of PPR, Pinault junior was faced with the familiar Scion challenge of leaving things as they were or putting his imprint on them. PPR was a conglomerate involved in building products, mail order and retail and had begun to make in-roads into luxury goods with the acquisitions of Gucci and Yves Saint Laurent. 'I was concerned that our assets were too closely tied to Western Europe, and to France in particular,' he said. 'The company needed to become more international, more growth-oriented, more profitable. So I focused on our luxury segment – apparel and accessories – which had strong potential for long-term growth.'[13]

Brands such as Brioni, Stella McCartney and Bottega Veneta were added to the portfolio, while the rest – including the Printemps department store and Fnac books and electricals stores – were exited. Pinault junior decided that getting bigger to fuel growth was not a strategy that would last forever. Instead, by 2014, group sales had declined by more than a half but profits were up by around 40 per cent. It was done without totally consigning what he inherited to the history books. Even the new name – Kering – attempted a nod backwards and forwards when it was announced in 2013, combining 'ker', meaning a house in the language spoken in Brittany, the north-western corner of France where the Pinault family hails from, and 'ing,' an indication of movement.

From different industries and different geographies, two more Scions that fit the evolutionary mould are Pansy Ho and James Murdoch. Ho is the eldest daughter of Stanley Ho, the casino mogul who turned the former Portuguese colony of Macau into Asia's gambling mecca whose revenues long ago eclipsed those of Las Vegas.

One of 17 children born to four wives, Ho marked herself out as the heir apparent by refusing to stand still when competition flocked to Macau as it came under Chinese rule in 1999. Instead of fighting against every American casino chain intent on breaking her family's

40-year monopoly, she partnered with one of them, striking a lucrative joint venture with MGM Resorts.

Speaking in a 2013 interview about her father's retreat from the operational side of the business, she said, 'My father is more obviously a leader who is respected by everybody, and he still provides his own views, but I think that the businesses are actually now quite independently run.'[14] Stanley Ho died in May 2020.

One of the best-known families in the media industry is the Murdochs, led by patriarch Rupert, who built an international news and entertainment empire from a clutch of Australian newspapers inherited from his father. The appointment in 2003 of his 30-year-old son James as chief executive of BSkyB, the UK satellite broadcaster, was tinged with controversy. Critics said Rupert, whose News Corporation at the time owned a 35 per cent stake in Sky, where he was chairman, had failed to listen to others who thought James was too junior for the role, even though he had previously been running the group's Star TV network in Asia.

Concerns were brushed off. What quickly became clear was that James was his father's son, attempting to inhabit the role of scrappy challenger taking on the might of the UK broadcasting establishment. Sky had launched in 1989 with four channels produced from a prefab structure in an industrial park on the fringes of west London but struck movie deals and captured football rights to entice viewers.

Investors with a short-term time horizon were looking forward to Sky hitting its long-held target of reaching eight million homes. Before it did so, in August 2004, Murdoch junior outlined plans to reach 10 million, accompanied by an investment plan that sent Sky shares slumping.

A year later, in October 2005, the takeover of internet service provider Easynet showed that Sky was intent on broadening its business model. Selling broadband subscriptions alongside its TV packages would vary its delivery mechanism but also take it into direct competition with another UK incumbent that Murdoch thought was ripe for disruption: telecoms provider BT. Murdoch junior ran the company with the same relentless attitude of his father, but gave it a modern spin and found new battles.

He stepped up to replace his father as Sky chairman in 2007 but departed the company under a cloud in 2012 when he was engulfed in the mobile phone hacking scandal at News International, the UK newspaper arm of the empire he was running at the time. Murdoch junior returned as Sky chairman in 2016 and the business was sold to US cable firm Comcast in a deal valued at £30 billion in 2018.

The family members are not always in lockstep, however. In January 2020, James Murdoch and his wife, Kathryn, issued a statement that criticized the way in which it said the family's news outlets had downplayed the impact of the global climate crisis while bushfires burnt across Australia. 'They are particularly disappointed with the ongoing denial among the news outlets in Australia given obvious evidence to the contrary,' a spokesperson said.[15] Since late 2018 James has had no day-to-day involvement in the family businesses and is making media investments through his own company, Lupa Systems.

Poured away

Less effective was the Scion leadership of the Seagram group. That corporate name is a historical relic now, but it used to be one of the world's leading drinks companies with brands including Chivas Regal whisky and Mumm champagne. It was built by an entrepreneurial Canadian, Samuel Bronfman, who sold whisky to US bootleggers during the prohibition era. After he died in 1971 the firm continued to expand under his son, Edgar senior. Dramatic changes took place under the third-generation leadership of Edgar junior from 1994 onwards.

The first sign that change was afoot came in April 1995 when Seagram sold the bulk of its 24 per cent stake in DuPont – the legacy of a takeover battle – back to the US chemicals group for $8.8 billion. Bronfman junior traded in the steady dividend generator to build an entertainment empire, first by acquiring film studio MCA in 1995 and later adding record label Polygram in 1998.

The younger Bronfmans clearly had an itch to scratch. Edgar senior had attempted a takeover of film studio MGM earlier in his career and his son had tried his hand as a film producer and lyricist. Edgar senior was mindful of how his father had looked over his shoulder when he was trying to lead the family firm in his way. Samuel had 'ruled by veto, not by imagination', Edgar senior said in one interview.[16] Consequently, Edgar junior was given his head regardless of some family misgivings.

Despite his deal making, Seagram, the drinks and media combine, lacked the scale of Disney or Time Warner so in June 2000 Edgar junior rolled the whole business into

Vivendi, a French water business that was also aiming to transform itself into an entertainment and internet giant. The timing of the all-paper deal looked good. After all, Seagram's share price had almost tripled in the five years since the DuPont disposal. But it was to prove disastrous as media and telecoms stocks crashed following the bursting of the dotcom bubble. Despite the disbandment of the drinks portfolio – sold off and split largely between rivals Diageo and Pernod Ricard for $8 billion – Vivendi's finances were in a parlous state from subsequent acquisitions made by the group's hard-driving Alpha chief executive Jean-Marie Messier.

It got messy. The Bronfmans campaigned for Messier's resignation but had already lost billions from their combined fortune by the time he left Vivendi in 2002. In late 2003, Edgar junior consoled himself with the $2.6 billion acquisition of Warner Music, one of the world's four major record labels at that time.

The family is far from broke today. But it is notable that the fears of the Founder known in the business as 'Mr Sam' came true. 'I'm worried about the third generation,' he said in an interview in 1966. 'Empires have come and gone.'[17]

Privilege and nepotism

The field of applicants for the role of Scion is a narrow one. It is the only leadership type in this book defined by birth. But those who are born to do it have to decide whether it is something for them. They are selected by their parents, their parents' advisers or the company board for high office. But they also get to test out whether this is the route for them over many years of preparation.

Scions have unique opportunities: insight at an early age into how corporations are run simply from listening at the dinner table, as well as a privileged education and sink-or-swim challenges thrown at them that a typical twenty-something graduate trainee would rarely be trusted with.

But grass roots understanding can be lacking. It is impossible for the Founder's son or daughter to truly learn the business from the ground up unless they are set a specific green-field task.

Gaining acceptance can be a struggle too. A Scion's success is taken for granted; their failure magnified. It is not easy to separate out a privileged background from the strategic foreground; their comfortable start versus what they have done with it. The best Scions are those that make thoughtful, successful leaders, no matter what their surname.

SCIONS IN BRIEF

Strengths: Deep understanding of a business gained over many years, excellent training, confident nature, passion, respect for tradition.

Weaknesses: Prone to extremes, either following the past too closely or departing from it.

Suitability: Leading the business they were born into. Otherwise, putting their money to work in different ways away from the glare of expectation, such as in philanthropy or venture capital.

Where you will find them: At or close to the helm of whatever their parents built before them.

Endnotes

This chapter: original Jean-François Decaux interview

1   JCDecaux (nd) Our founder. https://www.jcdecaux.com/group/
    our-founder (archived at https://perma.cc/ST38-D3K5)

2   Santander (2014) Ana Botín, unanimously appointed to chair the board
    of Banco Santander [Press Release] 10 September. https://www.
    santander.com/content/dam/santander-com/en/documentos/historico-
    notas-de-prensa/2014/09/NP-2014-09-10-Ana%20Bot%C3%ADn,%20
    unanimously%20appointed%20to%20chair%20the%20board%20
    of%20Banco%20Santander%20%20%20-en.pdf (archived at https://
    perma.cc/GNB3-XT7X)

3   Guillen, M F and Tschoegl, A (2008) *Building a Global Bank: The
    transformation of Banco Santander*, Princeton University Press, New Jersey

4   Kandell, J (2015) Ana Botín marks a new era at Banco Santander,
    Institutional Investor, 30 October. https://www.institutionalinvestor.
    com/article/b14z9yk99zywbj/ana-bot%C3%ADn-marks-a-new-era-at-
    banco-santander (archived at https://perma.cc/7YEY-NCBQ)

5   Ashton, J (2013) Small is beautiful, says Santander's Ana Botín, the
    Spanish banker with a desire for new lending, *Evening Standard*, 19
    April. https://www.standard.co.uk/business/markets/small-is-beautiful-
    says-santanders-ana-botin-the-spanish-banker-with-a-desire-for-new-
    lending-8579912.html (archived at https://perma.cc/DN3N-5FRU)

6   Ashton, J (2012) Lakshmi Mittal: Olympic flame could have gone on
    top of my Orbit, *Evening Standard*, 6 August. https://www.standard.co.
    uk/olympics/olympic-news/lakshmi-mittal-olympic-flame-could-have-
    gone-on-top-of-my-orbit-8009288.html (archived at https://perma.
    cc/7P4B-5MTG)

7   ArcelorMittal (2018) Aditya Mittal appointed President of
    ArcelorMittal [Press Release] 5 March. https://corporate.arcelormittal.
    com/media/press-releases/aditya-mittal-appointed-president-of-
    arcelormittal (archived at https://perma.cc/N2B6-4ESB)

8   The Focus (2017) Interview with Jacob Wallenberg, Investor AB,
    EgonZehnder, 1 January. https://www.egonzehnder.com/insight/
    jacob-wallenberg (archived at https://perma.cc/2LMZ-VFVB)

9   Ibid.

10 Ashton, J (2009) Rothermere: selling Standard like death of my parents, *The* Sunday *Times*, 15 February. https://www.thetimes.co.uk/article/ rothermere-selling-standard-like-death-of-my-parents-br232vp0xrj (archived at https://perma.cc/HMT6-NEXQ)

11 Harmsworth, V (nd) LinkedIn profile. https://www.linkedin.com/in/ vere-harmsworth-6099268b/?originalSubdomain=uk Linkedin (archived at https://perma.cc/W9EE-KGP2)

12 Pinault, F (2014) Kering's CEO on finding the elusive formula for growing acquired brands, *Harvard Business Review*. https://hbr. org/2014/03/kerings-ceo-on-finding-the-elusive-formula-for-growing- acquired-brands (archived at https://perma.cc/LX9L-XRNJ)

13 Ibid.

14 Ashton, J (2013) Wheels of fortune: Meet Pansy Ho, the billionaire behind Asia's gambling mecca in Macau, *Independent*, 13 April. https:// www.independent.co.uk/news/business/analysis-and-features/wheels-of- fortune-meet-pansy-ho-the-billionaire-behind-asias-gambling-mecca-in- macau-8570748.html (archived at https://perma.cc/Y9P2-WKTR)

15 Waterson, J (2020) James Murdoch criticises father's new outlets for climate crisis denial, *Guardian*, 14 January. https://www.theguardian. com/media/2020/jan/14/james-murdoch-criticises-fathers-news-outlets- for-climate-crisis-denial (archived at https://perma.cc/S69Y-KG46)

16 Milner, B (2006) The unmaking of a dynasty, *Cigar Aficionado*, 9 July. https://web.archive.org/web/20060709015412/http:/www. cigaraficionado.com/Cigar/CA_Profiles/People_Profile/0,2540,176,00. html (archived at https://perma.cc/8YGS-6TCV)

17 Burke, D (2002) The Bronfman saga From rags to riches to..., *Fortune Magazine*, 25 November. https://archive.fortune.com/magazines/ fortune/fortune_archive/2002/11/25/332573/index.htm (archived at https://perma.cc/7UWW-2GAT)

CHAPTER SIX

Lovers

Let's get physical

The throbbing music and red lights that studded the ceiling gave the room a nightclub air. Rows of toned torsos squatted and thrusted and swung weights, or lay on floor mats crunching their abs. Another column of keep-fit fanatics was pounding the treadmills lined up along each wall. The overwhelming feeling was of motion meets emotion, where physical pain segues into a soaring mental high.

At the centre of this physical exertion stood Joey Gonzalez, headset microphone clamped on and t-shirt encasing his impressive musculature. Constantly on the move – coaxing, twisting, bending – Gonzalez was taking part in the exercise class as enthusiastically as any club member as well as leading it like a pumped-up orchestra conductor.

He was also in his element. It does not take an endorphin rush to see that Gonzalez loves what he does. But although he fits right into these typical New York surroundings, he is not merely a gym instructor. Gonzalez is the chief executive of the entire company, Barry's Bootcamp – now called simply Barry's – one of the fastest-growing fitness studios of the past decade.

In a corporate world craving authenticity, companies swear blind they cannot survive without passion: for their product, for their customers and for their people. Yet this amorous drive has left passion as the most devalued word in corporate life. It is an immeasurable metric, but still succeeds as the one where leaders are most likely to fail. Yet there is a category of leader that does deliver passion in spades. Let's call them the Lovers – and they are far from faking it.

Their belief in what they do is deep-seated. Picking them out from bosses who merely play along at being interested in what their firm does is an easy task. They are enthusiasts for their product or service and the way of life it promotes. And that can feed into their career ambitions. They have no more desire than to do precisely what they are already doing. Compared with the promiscuity of Fixers or Sellers, who switch easily between industry sectors looking for their next challenge, these Lovers are loyal to the cause and have deep sector knowledge. Once they have identified their career passion they are likely to remain a one-industry man or woman for life.

School careers advice suggests doing something you love but few people manage it. These are the stories of the lucky few who love what they do and have managed to do it at the highest level. Like Gonzalez, the Lovers might have converted a hobby into a business. They might be a great user of the product they create and sell. Gareth Davis, once the chief executive of Imperial Tobacco, owner of cigarette brands including JPS, West and Davidoff, used to spark up at every opportunity, often in press conferences or stood outside afterwards. He wasn't doing it for effect: he really loves to smoke.

Those passions are bred young, which is why this chapter explores more than some of the others in this book where leaders acquire their motivations. The Lovers are likely to have grown up in their industry. There are trainees who return as leader to the companies that made them, such as Lord (Stuart) Rose, who in 2004 went back to the food and clothing retailer Marks & Spencer as chief executive after 15 years away. Or they could be someone who has scaled the ranks and never left in the interim, such as Steve Rowe, who started out as an M&S trainee in 1989 and was appointed chief executive in 2016.

Think of a player-manager in football, with a foot in both camps. They have unique understanding of the demands of the boardroom as well as the boot room – or, in the case of business, the factory or even the gym floor.

Cynics say it is easy to love something if you are paid circa £5 million a year and perhaps more when share incentives mature. But one of the strengths of this leadership type is their believability: they would be prepared to fill the role for far less. Nor do they have to explain at length how they got here. Their passion drew them in and they aren't going anywhere.

Gonzalez is one such Lover. It took 14 years from first walking into the original Barry's Bootcamp gym to becoming chief executive. In that time Barry's has won a reputation as the hottest fitness studio in town, attracting celebrity gym bunnies and regular fitness fans to a mix of cardio and weights training that promises great results.

Set up in 1998 in West Hollywood by the eponymous founder Barry Jay, it has grown to 80 outlets from Singapore to Stockholm and attracted numerous starry followers including Victoria Beckham, Harry Styles and Kim Kardashian along the way. Its first international foray was to Bergen in Norway in 2011 and London followed two years later.

In London in early 2018 to promote the opening of the fourth Barry's gym in the capital, it fast became clear Gonzalez didn't just lead the company. He embraced what it stands for. Clearly it wouldn't tally for a slob to lead the business, but for this Lover it informed his way of life and well-being. Sipping black coffee, the diminutive Gonzalez glowed with health, despite being on an incredibly challenging diet regime that meant he had sworn off sugar, alcohol, gluten and dairy and was fasting intermittently.

What began as a love of good health and fitness he had turned into his career, training as an instructor and then becoming chief executive of Barry's in 2015. Sometimes Lovers owe a debt of gratitude to the company they lead and that came across strongly in this case.

Gonzalez talked about how the business instilled him with a confidence that had previously ebbed away. His career, which had begun with a bang as a child actor, had been on the slide and he was drifting from job to job. Having walked into Barry's one day, it felt like home. Without sounding too schmaltzy, Gonzalez graduated from member to trainer and said that the first class he took 'was one of the best days of my life'.[1]

His private life was bound up in Barry's too. Gonzalez met his future husband Jonathan through the club. 'He was the first student I ever kissed,' he said. And, rather than leaving behind the gym floor for the executive suite, he keeps his hand in at the coal face. Gonzalez instructs classes on a Saturday morning, and, when the Covid-19 pandemic struck, he led virtual lessons on Instagram.

It is easy to imagine the fast-growing leisure industry is full of Lovers. Much simpler to rave about the experience of a holiday, a workout or a haircut than a factory widget or can of beans. For most chief executives it is enough to like your product, not love it. For some, being knowledge-able is sufficient to get the job done. It is rare that the biggest coffee chain is led by an award-winning barista or that a champion cyclist gravitates to the helm of bike retailer Halfords, for example. Neither of these skills read-ily lend themselves to being an effective leader. And that is what a Lover has to prove – that their passion enhances their capability, that their leadership results in a better business.

What a Lover does supply is a font of inspiration. Their enthusiasm is infectious, which means they should be able to get their workforce as well as other stakeholders on side with ease. The question is how to use this credibility and goodwill to inspire those around them to work hard and effect positive change.

Advertising passion

Before exploring that, it is worth mentioning marketing. There is no better way for a leader to convey to staff and customers they believe in the product than by fronting their own advertising campaign. At least that is what some Lovers believe. Jim Koch, the co-founder of the Sam Adams beer brand, appeared in his own company commercials for many years and came across as a credible Lover whose passion drove beer sales. The downside risk is that the boss comes over as cheesy, not authentic. Sellers would never dream of taking such a frontline role.

Perhaps the most famous leader to pursue this route is Victor Kiam, whose white hair, deep tan and gravelly voice became synonymous with selling electric razors in the early 1980s. Kiam had worked in sales and marketing at ladies underwear brand Playtex before embarking on a career as an entrepreneur. In the famous advertising campaign, he declared he had been so impressed by the Remington razor, 'I bought the company'.

But as he considered the deal at first, his wife Ellen pointed out that he had never used an electric razor in his life. Reportedly, his reply was, 'I've been selling brassieres for 13 years, and never worn one.'[2] His wife bought him a device the next day. Kiam compared it with the competing models and found Remington to be his favourite. The loss-making company turned a profit in Kiam's first year of ownership.

If driving sales is one upside, full-on corporate passion raises concerns over several possible downsides. Leaders who make a point of operating on the shop floor must ensure they still capture the respect of their peers. And passion can be a dangerous characteristic if it erodes objectivity and acts as a barrier to making tough decisions.

Gonzalez at Barry's might be treading a fine line but so far he has managed to make the correct business decisions to keep his membership happy. Also pleased – or so it appears – is the private equity group North Castle Partners which majority owns Barry's and was reported to be considering a $700 million sale of the business. That plan was scuppered by Covid-19 and in June 2020 Barry's announced an equity investment from the Los Angeles-based buyout firm LightBay Capital instead.[3]

Lovers must balance their passion with sufficient dispassion to get the job they love done. Their exceptional credibility with staff and customers suggests there is no one better to lead a company through a difficult patch. But what is not clear is how love and passion translate into taking the tough decisions that corporate life requires. It is no leadership at all to fail in the midst of a crisis.

Book lover

The mezzanine level of Waterstones' flagship bookshop in London's Piccadilly affords James Daunt a commanding view of his empire. Over the balcony he can gaze into the heart of the store, a cathedral devoted to the written word where books have been carefully sorted and neatly stacked so shoppers can glance easily from table to table.

In the other direction lies the back entrance of the establishment leading out to the genteel Jermyn Street and the shirt sellers TM Lewin and Aquascutum opposite. Directly below, Daunt can watch newcomers pause to look at posters, cards and collectables. Some of them will make a beeline for his vantage point: a coffee shop decorated with blonde, slatted wood that offers some respite from the hubbub downstairs and where delicious pastries are piled as carefully as the books.

In the age of Big Data, algorithms and computer cookies, this routine has still a part to play in sophisticated retail surveillance – and with added tea and cake. Daunt, suave, friendly, mild-mannered, thoughtful and appropriately bookish, prides himself on knowing his customer but it cannot hurt to know a little more. And although he sells books online, his biggest challenge since taking this job in 2011 has been to understand what it takes to be a bricks and mortar book retailer in the age of Amazon *et al.*

Waterstones' flagship store is Europe's largest bookshop. It boasts over eight miles of bookshelves in an art deco building a stone's throw from Piccadilly Circus that used to be the imposing Simpsons department store. But its prime location and proud boasts did not look like enough to save it not so long ago. The store was tatty and unloved, a place where passers-by were as likely to nip in to go to the loo as browse the paperbacks and actually buy something. Doomsayers were writing off the British brand, which traces its roots to 1982, as just another casualty of the High Street. Daunt changed that.

In that café one Friday afternoon in summer 2017, the revival was already underway. Six years into the job, the lifelong bookseller had lavished some tender loving care on the branches, installing comfy furniture, pyramid tables, fresh flowers and LED lighting. Crucially, he devolved power from head office and re-energized his army of knowledgeable staff by encouraging them to share their literary enthusiasm with customers. Together with a cost-cutting programme that reduced headcount, Waterstones bounced back into profit, making £10.9 million in the 2016 financial year. It proved not to be a one-off occurrence.

By definition, a passion project does not put profitability first. Except it must if the Lover at the helm understands that without solid profits there would not be anything left to be passionate about. Any turnaround specialist could have done as much with Waterstones, critics might say. But if he was a Fixer, in the business of mending corporations with a series of ruthless decisions, Daunt would have moved on by now. It was his passion as a book lover and, crucially, a book buyer that gave him extra perspective and the respect of his workforce to improve performance.

Daunt came over as a proud shopkeeper, gently arranging the displays as he navigated the floor where customers were browsing and hunting for gifts. In another life you could imagine he had just one shop, not hundreds. In another age, he would have been stood behind the counter in a perfectly starched apron. And that is almost how his story started.

Daunt's love of books was all-encompassing. His mother used to take him to the library every week in north London. Because his father travelled far and wide as a diplomat, an interest in travel reading was ignited too.

At the age of 25 he quit a career in investment banking – the prospect of which underwhelmed him – to follow his dream. It was not a cheap undertaking but he wanted to begin in some style so Daunt borrowed £240,000 to acquire a beautiful bookshop on Marylebone High Street in central London. He soon discovered it was the only job he ever wanted to do. He built Daunt Books into a collection of six shops dotted across London that became known for its intelligent staff and literary parties. And then Alexander Mamut came calling. The Russian billionaire, who had acquired Daunt's biggest rival Waterstones, wanted him to rescue the loss-making chain.

Daunt's revival story features numerous examples of doing things in the best interest of the business, not primarily the bottom line. One example is pulling back from selling space in its store fronts to publishers keen to promote their wares. At a stroke, Waterstones lost £27 million in income – not a wise move for any firm already struggling with profitability. Shoppers might not have noticed either. But it rebuilt some of the chain's swagger internally and aided Daunt's mission to encourage frontline staff to take ownership of their branch once again.

Daunt lives the brand. His mindset is that small is beautiful and there is room for all in the market, if they are good enough. Price, for many in the retail industry the primary consideration as the internet has driven greater transparency for the consumer, was a secondary consideration. 'I have been resolutely old-fashioned about it,' he confessed. 'We needed better shops.'[4] When he was an independent seller he had to battle for shelf space along with Waterstones and Borders. Waterstones versus Amazon is the same David and Goliath battle, he reasoned, but dramatically scaled up.

And now he is doing it again. This Lover is seeking to repeat the trick in the United States. Funds advised by Elliott, the US investment manager, acquired Waterstones from Mamut in 2018 and a year later added Barnes & Noble, the largest retail bookseller in the US. Daunt was appointed chief executive of both companies but relocated from London to New York to lead a revival of B&N, which has 627 stores and had been suffering from cutthroat digital competition. He described this latest deal as 'a very good day for bookselling'.[5]

There is an irony that hedge fund firm Elliott, which has a reputation for tough shareholder activism – it once had seized a ship that was owned by the Argentinian navy in a dispute over an outstanding bond payment – has become a saviour of the book trade. Perhaps it has been infected with some of Daunt's passion, which does not appear to be incompatible with making physical book retailers fit for the future.

Passion is sparked early. We know what we love, and leaders are no different. As a teenage music fan, Michael Rapino's passion stretched further than many. At the age of 15, he travelled 16 hours to savour his first gig – Robert Plant, the lead singer of Led Zeppelin. What marks Rapino out from other concertgoers is that he was more successful at running with his love and turning it into a wildly successful career.

Travelling long distances becomes second nature if you call home Thunder Bay, a city in the more sparsely populated part of Ontario, located on the Canadian side of Lake Superior. Little did Rapino know that his job would eventually take him to many more great gigs. One thing that wouldn't alter when he became a leader was the travelling.

Rapino took the helm in 2005 as president and chief executive of what was to become the world's biggest concert promoter. In 2020, a year when live music schedules were ravaged by Covid-19, Live Nation was slated to take US rockers The Eagles, Korean pop sensations BTS, Lady Antebellum, Cher, Sir Rod Stewart and many more on tour. In 2019, a year when annual revenues rose 7 per cent to $11.5 billion, it claimed to be the largest producer of live music concerts in the world, admitting nearly 98 million fans to more than 40,000 events for over 5,000 artists. Live Nation also has interests in famous venues including The Fillmore in San Francisco and the Ziggo Dome in Amsterdam; in the UK it runs the Reading and Leeds music festivals. It has evolved from a touring partner to a marketing partner for some of the biggest bands in the world.

In some ways Rapino was fortunate with his timing. After years of playing second fiddle to recorded music, concert tours were becoming the main event for acts struggling to monetize their work once CD sales began their decline. Of course, it is impossible to run a business on the scale of Live Nation on enthusiasm alone. The passion propelled him forward but it was no guarantee of success. What helped there is that Rapino is a stickler for the quality of the performance, concert facilities, food and drink and the slickness of the ticketing website. What is remarkable about him is that so early on he had set out plans to turn his hobby into his career. At the age of 21 he sketched out on a napkin how he wanted to run a giant live entertainment company by the time he turned 40. Dreams do not often come true like this, but having a sense of what that dream is is the first step to achieving it.

'I got lucky when I was a teenager when we were booking bands at university,' Rapino said. 'Those gigs were the greatest two hours in my life and there was nothing else I wanted to do. I knew my passion early, which is always the tough part of life, figuring out what makes you tick.'[6]

Rapino had worked in brewing, but was drawn to live events when Labatt, the Canadian beer company he worked for, invested in Canada's leading concert promoter. He is undoubtedly a Lover of music gigs and used to see 100 bands annually. It is fewer now as he criss-crosses the globe on business.

That passion is not diluted by commercial reality. His detractors say that more than anyone Rapino has industrialized the concert business. Today there are too many tours for music fans to keep track. But the biggest criticism of Live Nation is its pricing. Ticket prices for its amphitheatre and arena shows are up by double digits since 2017. The company says they are still competitive versus a night out to watch an NFL or NBA fixture. Lovers like Rapino well understand the passion for the live music experience – and that that is something fans are willing to pay top dollar for.

Strike oil

Alphas fall in love with the power their role bestows. And they are frequently in love with themselves. But Lovers fall in love with something different: if not the product, borne out of a youthful pastime, it is the day-to-day activity, the process, the competitive chase for business or the output that excites them.

It doesn't sound hard to get motivated, given the financial rewards for business success and the lifestyle that comes with it. If only it were that simple. These always-on demands, with stakeholders advancing from every angle, involve significant sacrifice, as described in earlier chapters. International leaders might find themselves on a plane for half of the year so that their body doesn't know what time zone it is in – and their family certainly don't have a clue.

Considering the stresses and strains, it is a special kind of leader who wears their responsibilities lightly. They leap out of bed very easily in the morning, eager to get on with it. 'I always like that Paul Getty quotation,' said Dame Cilla Snowball, a doyenne of the London advertising industry. 'Rise early, work late, and strike oil.'[7]

Advertising is a simple business. The best agencies produce great work that gets their client talked about in a positive way and – ideally – drives up sales. Yet many industry leaders fill it with smoke and mirrors. They argue their work is somehow more strategic or holistic than any agency that has gone before them. They might be passionate about their work, but these imagemakers aren't always authentic.

Dame Cilla took a more grounded view. She did not give the impression she was reinventing the wheel, just making sure it was well-oiled and roadworthy. The value of the creative work was of course very important but Dame Cilla realized early on that advertising was an industry that prospered on relationships. Whizzing from drinks reception to industry dinner, she prized those links over all else. Sporting bold colours and a smile permanently creased across her face, the success of Abbott Mead Vickers,

Britain's biggest advertising agency and part of the Omnicom network, was down in part to its ability to keep a string of flagship advertising clients for longer than anyone else in the industry thought possible.

In 2014, when Dame Cilla was arguably at the peak of her powers, AMV was sitting on client relationships of 30 years with *The Economist* magazine, 20 years with BT and heading towards 35 years with UK supermarket group Sainsbury's. It was the sort of relationship longevity of which only company auditors could boast – and regulators were scoping out how to encourage firms to put those contracts out to tender more often. But in the fickle world of advertising, where minds are changed as easily as some-one weighing up two different brands of washing-up liquid in the supermarket aisles on the weekly shop, the average client–agency relationship was just two-and-a-half years.

Of course, keeping these three cornerstone clients wasn't all down to Dame Cilla, but the boss-to-boss relationship cannot be underestimated. In an industry that was constantly striving to make its clients appear as authentic as possible, Snowball's high-energy enthusiasm and attention to detail were impossible to ignore. It encouraged those beneath her to pull out all the stops. Passion breeds better business.

It is also worth pointing out that she prospered in an industry that has not always been easy for women to fall in love with. The 1960s sexism portrayed in the *Mad Men* TV drama lingered on long after and wasn't far from the truth. Another leader, Stevie Spring, now chairman of the British Council, was advised to brush up on her shorthand when she joined the male-dominated agency world early in her career. Sometimes Spring missed meetings because they were scheduled to take place in men-only bars or at boxing matches.

Dame Cilla had been at AMV since 1992, chief executive since 2002 and chairman and chief executive of the wider AMV BBDO group since 2006. Just like Daunt and Gonzalez, she has been a one-industry person and mostly a one-company person too. Dame Cilla could have been there longer but it took her 11 years to join AMV after failing to get an interview for a job straight from university.

Every time a key account was put out to tender or a chief executive changed, she was on high alert. Often senior job changes can set off a chain reaction of new lieutenants and new suppliers. 'What we try and do is make sure our clients are actively selecting us, not passively inheriting us, because it is a very competitive world,' she said.[8] Dame Cilla's skill was to keep close to the top tier of each business just in case, but her attentiveness and friendliness were real.

Nothing is forever in advertising, an industry that is always striving to discover the next best thing. In 2016, Sainsbury's decided to go to another agency but AMV soon replaced it with rival chain Asda. In 2019, BT also opted to go elsewhere to relaunch its brand. Snowball, an authentic Lover, retired in 2018 having done more than most to nurture valuable relationships.

Strike gold

Mark Cutifani, the chief executive of diversified mining giant Anglo American, is another leader who sits squarely in this category. His love for his industry is obvious. Extracting great mineral wealth from some of the world's poorest regions in high-risk environments demands passionate, authentic leadership. The mining giants haven't always been able to offer that.

Cutifani has travelled the world running mines. These days he is suited and booted but this Australian is still more at home sporting a hard hat and overalls out on a site inspection than fielding questions back at base. He had to love the profession to get this far. To race through his engineering degree without denting his earnings, Cutifani worked night shifts in a mine and attended Wollongong University in New South Wales during the day.

After a career working in Toronto, Johannesburg and the deserts of Western Australia, he arrived to lead Anglo American in 2013 just as two big changes took place. Resources companies were facing tougher times after the growth in Chinese consumption of raw materials paused. And because the world's biggest miners had over-expanded, when sales growth slowed, they were saddled with billions of dollars in debt.

The method of leading this type of company had changed too. The history of Anglo American still loomed large. It had been set up a century earlier to exploit South Africa's precious metals deposits. From gold, it had gone on to produce copper, platinum and diamonds through ownership of De Beers, moving its primary stock market listing to London in 1999. But the days when colonial leaders could call the shots over the workers from a distant city were over. Mining was home territory for Alpha leaders, but Cutifani brought credibility with him as well as clout.

First of all this Lover needed to show that passion for what he did did not cloud the requirement to act dispassionately when tough action was called for. He might have dirt under his fingernails, but it did not stop him from putting 15 of Anglo's 69 mines up for sale in 2014, including many of its oldest South African platinum sites with long histories and sensitive industrial relations.

Cutifani was also clear that he needed to connect with the workforce, to show he cared. In his previous job, running gold miner AngloGold Ashanti, he attended the mass memorial held for striking workers shot during a wave of violence in the region. It was entirely appropriate that he did so – but he was the only mining chief to take that view. 'People are the business,' he said. 'The day you forget that the people are the ones that will make the real difference is the day you cease to be a leader.'[9]

Cutifani's passion was not going to halt progress. In fact, he used it to mobilize a significant programme of change. In a kind of 'war room' close to the entrance to Anglo's headquarters in London's St James's, he came across as a student of mining itching to put his ideas into practice.

Leaders love a sense of drama. If there isn't a burning platform, which a fire-fighting Fixer can expect as they arrive in a new role, sometimes they create one. This Lover's bunker wasn't full of quick fixes, however. The diagrams and text carried on the four walls spelled out longer-term ambitions: to conduct mining better by adopting some of the technology Cutifani had observed in adjacent industries that had yet to arrive in the dirty and dusty world of mineral extraction.

In the intervening years, that early ambition has solidified into a new way of working. Anglo's trademarked FutureSmart Mining led efforts to improve the way in which it operates its mines, by adopting greater precision to produce less waste, reducing dependency on water and making its facilities safer.

This plan could have been formulated by a strategist in a suit. But implemented by a Lover with a deep understanding of his industry at once lent it credibility and momentum. Cutifani has proved over time he is not afraid to do the difficult stuff, for the good of his shareholders but also for the good of his people.

Giving more

It makes sense that numerous Lovers occupy the not-for-profit space. Kick away the bumper payday and profit imperative and leaders focus even more on what they are passionate about. Beccy Speight is a case in point. In 2019, she became chief executive of the Royal Society for the Protection of Birds, a familiar brand in the UK whose scale is often underestimated.

The RSPB is the largest conservation organization in Europe, with more than 1.2 million members, over 2,000 employees and a socking 12,000 volunteers. It also maintains over 200 nature reserves which are home to 80 per cent of the UK's rarest or most threatened bird species. Its role in preserving the UK's natural resources is critical.

Speight's appointment wasn't a surprise. She had been hired to the 130-year-old charity from the Woodland Trust where she had been chief executive since 2014. Before Royal Dutch Shell and every other corporation feeling guilty they were not doing enough for the environment pledged to plant millions of trees, the Woodland Trust had already gained traction for its campaign to plant 50 million trees right across the north of England to create a new 'Northern Forest'. Speight was a UK charity leader to watch.

Her love of the natural world went right back to childhood. 'I grew up in Dorset and we were always camping or fishing or wandering off up dry riverbeds so I very much grew up with that,' she said. 'I remember long wildflower walks thinking this is very dull but actually learning quite a lot. That was always with me.' She studied English instead of geography and eventually became a management consultant. 'The buzz was fantastic but I just got to the stage where it wasn't enough for me. I wanted to do something that felt like it really mattered and for me that was getting back into the natural environment and trying to fight the big fight that I think is going on over that at the moment.'[10]

That led to 14 years spent at the National Trust, rising to become director for the Midlands region. 'The attraction of the role for me is that the RSPB is of a scale and of a steely determination to make a difference to the biggest issues facing us today, which are climate change and the loss of species. I wanted to be somewhere where I could make the most difference with my little bit of time,' she added.

Tough love too

Lovers are one of the most important leadership types to have emerged in recent years. They are very nearly the full package. Far more than just professional managers, they have a genuine, personal connection with the organization they lead. That can be hugely powerful in celebrating a brand, motivating others and spreading their own passion to the workforce.

Lovers tend to be good communicators willing to enthuse about their favourite subject but their authenticity means that deeds trump words: they don't need to convince anyone about what they believe in. They are not advancing their own agenda, the only thing on their mind is allegiance to the cause and to their staff. That single-minded focus means they are less likely to have picked up numerous non-executive roles to clutter their diary. There is little evidence that a lack of ambition to find their next role makes them too comfortable to perform. Tough love is not absent when required.

The only question is how passion is put to work. Some Lovers need to pair their passion with a purpose, to do more with the allegiance and confidence they inspire. For that, they could take a lesson from the next leadership type, the Campaigners.

LOVERS IN BRIEF

Strengths: Deep passion for and knowledge of their industry. Authenticity that breeds staff loyalty.

Weaknesses: Perhaps they could drive their business harder. Risk of failing to take tough decisions.

Suitability: People businesses that need an engaged, empathetic figurehead.

Where you will find them: Wherever they really, really want to be.

Endnotes

1   Ashton, J (2018) Barry's Bootcamp CEO Joey Gonzalez is the man who can get anyone ripped, *Evening Standard*, 25 January. https://www. standard.co.uk/lifestyle/london-life/joey-gonzalez-ceo-of-barrys-bootcamp-interview-and-lifestyle-a3749561.html (archived at https://perma.cc/VT8A-7X2M)

2   Barker, D (2001) Victor Kiam Obituary, *Guardian*, 30 May. https://www.theguardian.com/news/2001/may/30/guardianobituaries (archived at https://perma.cc/E84T-5AMD)

3   Tan, G (2020) Barry's Bootcamp gets equity investment from LightBay Capital, *Bloomberg*, 18 June. https://www.bloomberg.com/news/articles/2020-06-18/barry-s-bootcamp-gets-equity-investment-from-lightbay-capital (archived at https://perma.cc/4HSY-HKZ5)

4   Ashton, J (2017) Bookshops are back: Waterstones' boss says younger readers have helped open a new chapter for high street stores, *Mail on Sunday*, 10 June. https://www.thisismoney.co.uk/money/news/article-4591612/Waterstones-boss-says-young-readers-helped-grow.html (archived at https://perma.cc/U84J-FQK9)

5   Business Wire (2019) Elliott completes acquisition of Barnes and Noble, 7 August. https://www.businesswire.com/news/home/20190807005399/en/Elliott-Completes-Acquisition-Barnes-Noble (archived at https://perma.cc/EQ9S-545Y)

6   Ashton, J (2014) The ticketmaster: 23,000 events, 60 million attendees, $6.5 billion sales – meet Michael Rapino, the man behind Live Nation, *Evening Standard*, 10 March. https://www.standard.co.uk/lifestyle/london-life/the-ticketmaster-23000-events-60-million-attendees-65-billion-sales-meet-michael-rapino-the-man-9181317.html (archived at https://perma.cc/TX6R-DDMX)

7   Ashton, J (2014) Interview: Cilla Snowball – the woman tasked with helping London's Mad Men sell themselves, *Evening Standard*, 18 July. https://www.standard.co.uk/business/markets/interview-cilla-snowball-the-woman-tasked-with-helping-london-s-mad-men-sell-themselves-9614276.html (archived at https://perma.cc/F6CB-79VC)

8   Ibid.

9   Ashton, J (2014) Interview: Mark Cutifani – D-Day looms for rough diamond as he digs Anglo American out of a hole, *Evening Standard*, 21 November. https://www.standard.co.uk/business/markets/interview-mark-cutifani-d-day-looms-for-rough-diamond-as-he-digs-anglo-american-out-of-a-hole-9874771.html (archived at https://perma.cc/K5Z5-6KPC)

10 Ashton, J (2019) Leading with James Ashton S2 Episode 6 – Entrepreneur First and RSPB, *Apple Podcasts*, 18 November. https://podcasts.apple.com/gb/podcast/s2-episode-6-entrepreneur-first-and-rspb/id1460796936?i=1000457108392 (archived at https://perma.cc/SQ6H-7G3L)

CHAPTER SEVEN

Campaigners

Making business pay

When Ajay Banga moved to New York in 2000 his career
was on a roll. After four years at Citigroup, spent largely
in London and Brussels, this latest promotion maintained
the momentum that had begun when he started out as a
management trainee for Nestlé in his native India 19 years
earlier. Before long, dispatched east to lead the Asia-Pacific
region, he would be talked of as a potential leader of the
investment bank.

But even though Banga had a high-paying role at one of
Wall Street's best-known institutions, there was a problem.
He was astonished to discover that his lack of US credit
history severely impacted his ability to put down roots.

'I couldn't rent an apartment, I couldn't get a phone,' he said, recalling those days. 'Life was pretty crazy.'

Banga recalls wandering the streets of Manhattan trying to get connected. In an AT&T store he handed over his new social security number to a young man behind the counter – who coincidentally also had South Asian roots – only to be told it wasn't enough.

'I looked at him and said, "Listen man, I grew up in India, I have worked overseas, this is the job I do. How the heck can you not give me a cellphone?" I didn't believe it. The young guy replied, "I need some proof that you are actually worth some money."'

Banga returned soon after with a statement from Smith Barney that detailed the private brokerage account he had set up while living in London. He remembers the shop assistant taking one look at it and with a laugh, saying, 'You have too much money not to have a credit history.' Still, it took several hours to get back-office approval as details of Banga's wealth were shuttled between administrators before he obtained his handset. Renting an apartment was even more complicated and required a letter of guarantee from Citigroup.

These incidents were a minor taste of what would become a major issue for the man who went on to become president and chief executive of the financial services giant Mastercard in 2010. Years later, and on several occasions, Banga raised the complexities of settling in the United States with those high up in the US government. 'Our system is not built for immigrants, our system is built for those already here and that is a form of exclusion that I find reprehensible,' he said.

Banga made financial exclusion a key theme of his decade-long leadership of Mastercard, one of the world's most instantly recognized brands that adorns billions of credit and debit cards and processes payment transactions between merchants and banks. What he had in mind was far more than merely helping out mildly inconvenienced New York bankers.

The financially included are the banked majority: those members of the global money system that can transact and save with ease. The ambition is to bring inside the rest of the populace, opening up access to a bank account or electronic wallet that allows them to store money digitally and send and receive payments for the first time. It is a passport to a different world, a first step towards managing a family's finances, taking advantage of other financial services such as credit and insurance, and even starting a business or investing in education.

Taken together, these measures are proven to boost quality of life, reduce poverty and encourage economic growth. The principal beneficiaries are women. Around the world, only 69 per cent of adults have their own account and 1.7 billion remain unbanked, according to the Global Findex database in 2017.[1] Although these figures are a sharp improvement on a decade ago, it is still shocking that a Federal Deposit Insurance Corporation survey in 2017 found that 14 million Americans did not have a bank account.[2] One of the reasons the numbers are improving is that Mastercard set a target in 2014 to connect at least 500 million people outside the financial mainstream by 2020. This mission became synonymous with Banga the Campaigner.

Campaigners believe their remit extends beyond driving corporate performance to deliver purpose alongside profit. They stick their neck out and use their company as a platform from which to project a vision of equality, diversity or a greener world. They risk their reputation, speaking passionately for a cause, often committing shareholder funds to doing good deeds. They often have the passion of Lovers, discussed in the previous chapter, but seek to ball that up into something bigger.

A generation or so ago, leaders led campaigns to develop the best product or outsell the competition. Today these Campaigners' outlook appeals to millennial workers for whom the size of the pay cheque is only part of the recruitment package, plus consumers who care about doing the right thing. Politicians, too, favour firms that benefit the broader community in which they operate.

Some Campaigners believe they are visionaries; others are far humbler. But neither should be mistaken for Greta Thunberg in pinstripes. They must alight on causes with enlightened self-interest: something that is good for business and the wider world – and, cynically, perhaps also themselves. In a world drowning in thought leadership, the challenge is to turn big ideas into concrete action, without neglecting the bottom line. And they must do it credibly, conscious that multi-millionaire eco-warriors don't always strike the right tone.

At Citigroup from 1996, Banga stumbled into microfinancing and began to understand that small money flows could have a large impact. A colleague was securitizing loans for Brac, an international development organization based in Bangladesh. It meant that transactions as low as a handful of dollars could be bundled together so that banks that typically dealt in sums far larger could deal in them.

'I began to understand how important it was for these institutions to free up their balance sheet so they could keep doing the work they were doing,' he said. Banga also read *The Fortune at the Bottom of the Pyramid*, a 2004 book by the Indian academic CK Prahalad that made the case for encouraging entrepreneurialism among the world's poorest as a method of eradicating poverty.

'I also understood there is not enough money in philanthropy and government in the world to solve our problems. That means we have to put private sector capital, ingenuity and technology to work,' he added.

Beginning at Mastercard in 2009, Banga could not figure out how this developing ambition fitted with the firm's business model. Mastercard already had a charitable foundation, created at the time of the group's initial public offering (IPO), which invested in education programmes in developing markets. But Banga knew he could not mix business with philanthropy.

An early partnership with the South African Social Security Agency (SASSA) showed him the way. Mastercard helped to digitize a system of cash benefits that was cumbersome and prone to fraud. In a four-month period during 2012, a newly issued debit card for grant payments was credited with driving up South Africa's banked population from 63 per cent to 67 per cent. By summer 2013 there were 10 million active cards in the programme.

Banga set about doing more. What this campaign needed now was a target. That came in 2014, at the World Bank and International Monetary Fund (IMF) spring meetings, an annual pow-wow of central bankers, politicians and leaders from business and civil society discussing the state of the world.

Banga was due to share a stage to talk about financial inclusion with World Bank president Jim Yong Kim, IMF chief Christine Lagarde and Queen Maxima of the Netherlands, the United Nations' special advocate on the topic. Before they went out, Queen Maxima urged Banga to give some sense of the scale of Mastercard's ambition. Unplanned, mid-way through the discussion, he announced the 500 million target.

'I think she almost fell off the stage,' he said, referring to Queen Maxima. 'There are photographs that show us both laughing hysterically. She said to me, "I only expected 50 million. Are you crazy?" It was a hairy target but it worked out.'

With the objective formally unveiled a year later as a Universal Financial Access commitment, Mastercard had clear impetus from the top and something to be measured against. Whenever Banga took to the stage at a conference somewhere in the world, he was invariably asked about his campaign. But beneath the grand sweeping gesture there was no single scheme designed to make a vast difference. Instead, 750 financial inclusion programmes grew up in more than 80 countries to tackle the challenges of income equality. Rather than wielding a stick in markets with low penetration, Mastercard dangled carrots that offered numerous reasons for the unbanked to sign up.

For example, in Egypt the company pioneered a method for women to receive alimony payments on their card so they no longer had to go into a bank branch and identify as a divorcee. In East Africa in 2017, the digital platform

2KUZE was developed to connect smallholder farmers, agents, buyers and banks. In Kenya and Tanzania, most farmers might tend no more than a couple of acres of land and until they began transacting on their phones, would otherwise have had to walk hours to market to find a buyer for their produce. Mastercard's target was accomplished early and increased to 1 billion by 2025, something for Banga to keep an eye on, having moved up to become group chairman in January 2021.

This Campaigner was successful in his own right, but also fortunate to have landed at a company like Mastercard. Here was a fast-growing and extremely profitable enterprise – much more so when Banga had finished running it. In 2019, net revenues rose 16 per cent to $16.9 billion and net income was up 42 per cent at $8.1 billion. Mastercard had $9 billion of cash and cash equivalents sitting on its balance sheet. It committed $500 million to financial inclusion, a not inconsiderable sum, but it could afford to do good.

It also had international reach. The group's customers had 2.6 billion cards in issue – although many of them were not physical cards – and gross transaction volumes amounted to $6.5 trillion. It had a global network across which it could defray technology investment and good local understanding of what each market needed.

It is also important to acknowledge Mastercard's back story. The business began life in 1966 as a credit card association of US banks and only struck out independently in 2006. In that year it converted into a private company and sold shares on the New York Stock Exchange, which at the time was the 12th-largest domestic IPO in US history. It used to be the place 'where bankers went when they were sent to pasture', Banga pointed out in an interview at Goldman Sachs in 2019. 'It was not a bad life.'[3]

The co-operative of thousands of financial institutions was also grouped into regional fiefdoms all around the world, using a patchwork of systems. Banga's predecessor, Robert Selander, made great strides to mesh all this together into a single entity but by the time he took the helm it was still a company figuring out its culture and beliefs. Financial inclusion was a timely campaign, but also a unifying force.

Banga judged it well. He made sure that Mastercard was not acting alone. His campaigning spirit carried others along with it, inside the company and out. Mastercard worked in partnership with governments and international development organizations. For example, in East Africa 2KUZE was piloted with the Cafédirect Producers Foundation and developed with the help of a grant from the Bill & Melinda Gates Foundation.

Of course, nor was financial inclusion completely altruistic. Jousting with its arch rival Visa to be the pre-eminent global payments system, Mastercard clearly wanted to recruit as many new customers as possible. Additionally, Banga was mindful of the plethora of fintech start-ups that threatened his business model – and that the real enemy they were united against was cash. But those newly included sign-ups will be largely loss-making for a long time to come.

'Commercially sustainable does not necessarily mean immediately profitable,' Banga said. 'It just means that if you were to be investing in this for a period of time it would at the end of the day enable your business to be better run, better managed and more profitable for you and those who you work with.'

Banga successfully united a good cause with investment in Mastercard's future while continuing to drive up returns. Not all Campaigners have a credit history of which they can be so proud.

Feed the world

In 2009, the same year that Ajay Banga joined Mastercard, Paul Polman arrived at Unilever, home to the familiar Lipton tea, Dove soap, Ben & Jerry's ice cream and Knorr soup brands that line supermarket shelves the world over. Polman, who had spent 26 years at Procter & Gamble before a brief sojourn at Nestlé, knew the consumer goods industry inside out. He also knew his own mind. The Dutchman had little interest in leading a group that merely fulfilled the short-term requirement of keeping shareholders happy with solid sales growth and dependable dividends. Boldly, one of his first significant moves was to ditch the quarterly financial guidance shared with the stock market to assure investors that all was going to plan.

The following year he was even bolder – and not just because at a high-profile public gathering he dared to drink a glass of water taken straight from the River Thames. In November 2010, Polman made a statement about Unilever's future but also about the man who was leading the business. Launched with events in London, Rotterdam, New York and Delhi, Unilever's Sustainable Living Plan (SLP) would colour much of his time in office over the next decade.

Aligned to many of the United Nations' development goals, this scheme aimed to improve the health and well-being of more than a billion people, improve the livelihoods of people in Unilever's supply chain and prove that it was possible to grow sustainably over the coming decade without the company increasing its impact on the environment. Polman wanted to demonstrate that Unilever could have a resolutely positive impact, such as with its water purifying system Pureit, which made murky river water safe to consume.

There were targets to boost the nutritional value of Unilever's food, link an extra 500,000 small farmers and distributors in developing markets to its supply chain, and halve the water use associated with its products. What was revolutionary was that the initiative covered not just the group's own environmental footprint but those of its suppliers and consumers too. Polman assessed that its corporate might could be used to change behaviours far beyond its own production lines and office towers, so that, for example, purchasers of its shampoos took shorter showers to save water.

The big question was whether this mission was compatible with delivering for shareholders as well as the planet. Piling the pressure on itself, Unilever also aimed to double group sales over the same 10-year timeframe.

'We do not believe there is conflict between sustainability and profitable growth,' Polman the Campaigner wrote in the SLP launch document. 'The daily act of making and selling consumer goods drives economic and social progress.

There are billions of people around the world who deserve the better quality of life that everyday products like soap, shampoo and tea can provide.'4

This wasn't wholly new territory for Unilever. Its pursuit of profit with a purpose can be traced back to its founding father Lord Leverhulme, who built homes for his soap factory workers at Port Sunlight on the Wirral more than a century ago. Rather than sharing profits, Leverhulme termed as 'prosperity sharing' the idea of giving staff decent and affordable houses, amenities and welfare provisions. Founded in 1888, the village, which is home to more than 900 Grade II listed buildings set in 130 acres of parkland and gardens, still stands today.

It is rare that the modern Campaigner builds houses for its workers – although Google chief executive Sundar Pichai has driven deeper into property development to ease the housing crisis affecting many in the group's home town of San Francisco. Instead, most modern Campaigners go further in other ways. Now 'prosperity sharing' covers trying to do the best for their staff but also for those their company touches in the wider community.

Polman was a unique type of leader: a Campaigner first with some very novel ideas but very nearly an old-school Alpha because of the way he drove their delivery. Tall, imperious, talkative, worldly; he was as likely to be taking to the stage at the World Economic Forum in Davos, Switzerland, or the United Nations in New York as actually running his business.

The impassioned Polman – who might have become a priest after studying at a Carmelite seminary – brought a religious fervour to his method of business leadership that won him as many critics as admirers. His sustainability plan powered his regime in a way that, outwardly, a fascination with product development, sales and marketing did not.

It also powered his profile. If the aim is to influence others, campaigns rarely work unless they are publicized. By definition, a higher proportion of Campaigners frequent media channels to talk about their cause. But Polman was very conscious that his campaigning was at the behest of shareholders. 'If I don't have the business results, the guns will come out very quickly,' he admitted in 2013, four years into his reign, by which point Unilever's share price had doubled.[5]

Polman stands as a leader who bundled up so much into one mission statement. Chief executives had been nudged to do more for years by some branches of the investment community. In the UK, the 1999 revision of the Pensions Act meant that pension fund trustees had to declare to what extent they took social and environmental considerations into account in their investment policies. On the broader stage a year later, the UN launched its Global Compact to encourage bosses to follow sustainable policies in areas from anti-corruption to human rights.

Doing good while doing well was a nice idea that did not deliver often enough. Corporate social responsibility (CSR) policies gave way to socially responsible investing (SRI) and then environmental, social and governance (ESG) practices. The acronyms paid off only if the leader of the business bought into what they were aiming for. Too often good works were buried in the business and were disconnected from its main aims.

The breakthrough came when companies and investors understood they could champion causes that also increased their value. They also realized they should. Campaigners at the helm were not just accepted but to some extent expected. In the United States in 2006, a not-for-profit organization was set up to accredit companies that were a force for good. B Lab was created by three friends – Andrew Kassoy, Jay Coen Gilbert and Bart Houlahan – who left their careers in business and private equity hoping to make a difference to society. So far there are more than 2,500 certified B Corps – beneficial corporations – in over 50 countries, whose social and environmental performance has been judged to meet high standards.

Such momentum put ESG squarely in the mainstream. In August 2019, the US Business Roundtable, a group of chief executives from major US corporations chaired by Jamie Dimon, the chairman and chief executive of Wall Street banking giant JPMorgan Chase, could not have been more explicit. It committed to enhancing stakeholder value in place of shareholder value – a momentous shift if words are backed up by deeds.

In February 2020, the new chief executive of BP, Bernard Looney, set a target to reduce the oil firm's carbon footprint to net zero by 2050. His credentials as a Campaigner were established before investors really knew his corporate strategy – although any gentle bedding-in was curtailed by an oil price collapse courtesy of a power struggle between the US and Saudi Arabia and falling demand during the Covid-19-inspired lockdown. Cynicism aside, if this is how one of the biggest companies in the UK is run now – where a sense of mission trumps shareholder returns – the Campaigner's time has come.

But events late in Polman's tenure at Unilever were a reminder of the delicate balancing act these crusaders must maintain. An unwanted takeover approach threw fresh attention on his campaigning ways. In early 2017, Kraft Heinz proposed a merger with Unilever that would have forged a new grocery giant from two very different corporate cultures. Compared with Unilever's mission to feed the world, Kraft had been a vehicle that fed investors. It was bankrolled by 3G Capital, a buyout house founded by three Brazilian dealmakers, plus legendary investor Warren Buffett. Their model of buying up assets in low-growth industries such as packaged food and aggressively squeezing costs could not be further from Polman's ideal.

The approach failed, but it led to questions being asked about Polman's tactics. If he had been running Unilever more aggressively himself, perhaps the underperforming spreads business – including brands Blue Band and Flora – might have been hived off sooner. By the end of 2017 it was sold to private equity firm KKR for €6.8 billion. And a year after that, Polman announced he was retiring.

There was another misstep on the way. Unilever's declaration in March 2018 that it was replacing its dual shareholder structure – a legacy of the merger of Lever Brothers with Margarine Unie of the Netherlands in 1930 – with a single legal entity and primary share listing in Rotterdam was eventually defeated by UK shareholders who did not want the stock to be lost from the FTSE 100, which many of their funds followed. This, said his critics, was down to Polman's failure to read investors because his focus was elsewhere.

Meanwhile the Sustainable Living Plan has recorded mixed results. Progress by 2019 showed that Unilever had beaten its target on health and hygiene, reaching not just 1 billion but 1.3 billion people, helping to reduce diarrhoea through increased handwashing among other initiatives. But consumer water use associated with its products, which was intended to halve by 2020, had actually risen by 1 per cent since 2010. And, as long ago as its 2015 progress report, Unilever pushed out by a decade its target of halving the greenhouse gas impact of its products across their lifecycle.

'Large-scale systems transformation is needed to drive change faster on our greenhouse gas target in particular,' the company explained.[6] In other words: we can't do this on our own. Polman might be able to talk round politicians and investors to see his point of view, but consumers, who typically generate two-thirds of the greenhouse emissions for Unilever's products – such as by heating water for washing – have been slower to change.

Whether a campaign needs to succeed for the Campaigner who conceived it to be seen as successful is a moot point. Setting a 'hairy' goal to coalesce around – as Ajay Banga did at Mastercard – fuels the debate, marshals the troops, gets the peer group thinking and begins positive action. It also sets up a Campaigner to be shot at. By insisting their organization should do good – and by implication that others should do better too – they attract critics and the suspicion that acute financial discipline is not at the top of their agenda.

Polman would have been sacked if Unilever's finances had veered sharply off track; he would never have been ousted for failing to cut water usage or carbon emissions. 'I always say I represent one of the biggest NGOs (non-governmental organizations),' Polman said at one event in 2016, demonstrating where his mind was.[7]

Speaking at a virtual stakeholder event in May 2020 held to mark the plan entering its final year, Alan Jope, Polman's successor as chief executive from January 2019, said, 'The Unilever Sustainable Living Plan was a game-changer for our business. Some goals we have met, some we have missed, but we are a better business for trying. It has required immense ingenuity, dedication and collaboration to get to where we are now. We have made very good progress, but there is still more to do.'[8]

The company admitted that sometimes measuring impact – such as of its efforts to improve life chances for women – had proved difficult. But it said the SLP had helped it to hire strong talent. And it flagged that coming next was Unilever Compass, a 15-year successor strategy based on the beliefs that 'brands with purpose grow, companies with purpose last, and people with purpose thrive'. Polman's campaigning legacy lives on.

Credible campaigning

Some companies are consumed by purpose. So are their leaders. Founders who are also Campaigners can ensure that is the case because they set the terms by which their firm is run. In fact, the cause at the heart of their organization could be why it was set up in the first place. Profits don't power purpose; all along the purpose was hunting for a profit centre to sustain it.

California-based outdoor clothing firm Patagonia, famous for its fleece jackets and rainwear, donates 1 per cent of sales to environmental causes. It has been known to close down its stores and offices so staff – including Rose Marcario, the chief executive until June 2020 – could join in climate protests. And it has anti-capitalist tendencies, such as encouraging its loyal customer base to get their garments repaired instead of simply buying a replacement. In 2018, Marcario founded Time To Vote, a neutral coalition committed to increasing voter participation in US elections that attracted nearly 500 companies to its cause.[9]

She was in lockstep with the founder Yvon Chouinard, who was a rock climber when he established Patagonia in 1973. Although the privately held company is already doing more for the environment than many of its peers, Chouinard wanted to accelerate its efforts as the climate crisis became more acute. In December 2018, the group introduced a sharper mission statement: 'We're in business to save our home planet.' Chouinard also advised his human resources team that whenever an opening emerged in the company they should hire the person most committed to saving the planet.[10]

Toms Shoes also figured out a sustainable symbiosis. The man who would become the Campaigner at the helm, Blake Mycoskie, saw the hardship faced by children growing up without shoes while he was travelling in Argentina. His business hardwired doing good alongside doing well. For every pair of shoes sold, Toms donated a pair to someone in need. Thanks to his much-copied 'One for One' model, more than 86 million pairs have been given to children since 2006 and the group has expanded into sunglasses and coffee.[11]

Proof positive that Mycoskie had bridged the divide between profit and purpose came in 2014 when private equity group Bain Capital bought a 50 per cent stake in a deal that valued the enterprise at $625 million. But evidence that doing good did not guarantee doing well followed in 2019 when Toms was taken over by its creditors as outstanding loans caught up with it amid signs consumers were tiring of the concept.[12]

Campaigners who aren't Founders must tread more carefully. It is not harder to make their mark, just different. In both cases they can be so far ahead of the curve in identifying a new cause or method of helping as to be ridiculed. But it doesn't mean they aren't right in the end. A good example is provided by Jochen Zeitz and how what he was talking about a decade ago has shot up the corporate and environmental agenda.

Fast feet

Jochen Zeitz made his name by overhauling Puma, the running shoe brand, where he was chairman and chief executive for 18 years until 2011. On a shoestring budget, Zeitz restored the excitement about the brand that had been worn by legendary Brazilian footballer Pelé, focusing on cheaper African teams and athletes that underscored a spirit of adventure to take sales from Nike and Adidas. Rather fortuitously, that involved signing up a young Usain

Bolt, who would go on to become a world record-holding sprinter.

But it is what else Zeitz did that has really set the tone for the rest of his career. He put sustainability front and centre of the Puma revival. Short of resources, it wasn't a call that every chief executive would have made, and nor was it capitalized on as a marketing ploy to sell more shoes. Zeitz devised an environmental profit-and-loss account that set out what the company's air pollution, land use, water use and carbon consumption cost the planet, first published in his last year at the helm.

'With this, we treat our environment as an equal partner who bills us for providing clean water and air, restoring soils and the atmosphere, and decompose waste,' Puma says today.[13]

It must have been easier for the group to champion this approach because it was not the market leader. Like many challenger brands, it was prepared to experiment as it searched for a point of difference. And Zeitz's original outlook could have stemmed from his age. He was only 29 when he was promoted to run Puma in 1993. He joined the business as a marketer after returning to his native Germany from a job in New York with Colgate-Palmolive.

Zeitz understood that the secret to being a successful Campaigner was to hunt for wins on all sides. Any product-creating, staff-employing, profit-generating firm has a wide range of stakeholders. There was also a sense of trial and error in his approach.

'You know it is not one thing that will ultimately move it along, it is the combination of a lot of things,' Zeitz said, sandy-haired, cool as a cucumber with rugged rock star looks. 'The more we try to find tangible solutions to the problems the bigger the chance of actually finding them.'[14]

And then the key for any effective Campaigner is to own their mission, just as Polman and Banga have done. The idea that running shoes would one day detail the 'environmental calories' consumed in making them on the side of the box – similar to how cereal packets list sugar and salt content – seemed a little far-fetched when it was announced. But Zeitz confidently thought it was the right thing to do. He calculated that one stakeholder group, investors, would start to care when another group, consumers, did. And they have in great numbers.

The fashion industry is responsible for 10 per cent of all carbon emissions, more than international flights and maritime shipping combined.[15] Clothes makers who have rapidly increased production and the number of ranges they put out each year are under pressure to rethink the business model. Consumers are going on clothing fasts by pledging not to buy anything new for their wardrobe for a year.

After stepping back from his Puma leadership role in 2011, Zeitz worked more broadly for Kering, the French luxury goods house that acquired the sneaker maker. He introduced environmental profit and loss for many of Kering's brands – which include Alexander McQueen and Gucci – and gave the impression that full-time work got in the way of his mission. 'Being able to dedicate 100 per cent of my time to impacting more businesses without being operational, it just gives me a bigger platform,' he added, in a conversation in 2015.[16]

He also helped Harley-Davidson develop an electric bike and reared endangered species on his 50,000-acre Kenyan ranch, Segera. With Sir Richard Branson, he launched The B Team, a group of business leaders including the Indian industrialist Ratan Tata, who believed there was more to corporate life than Plan A, the relentless pursuit of profit.

Puma, in comparison, did not initially perform so well financially. By 2013 it was not hitting financial targets despite a string of high-profile sponsorships. By 2018, when the parent company Kering spun it off in a bid to focus on high-end luxury brands, it was faring better. In five years, the group's gross profit margin lifted from 46.5 per cent to 48.4 per cent and underlying earnings had gone from €191 million to €337 million.

Over the same period, Puma's environmental profit-and-loss value fell by 13.6 per cent as a proportion of revenue – meaning the brand had significantly reduced its impact on the planet.[17] In this instance, the Campaigner did well in the aftermath of leading a company so memorably. So did the company he left behind. It is difficult to prove that profit boosts purpose or vice versa – whether a bigger surplus means that sustainability efforts are redoubled or an environmentally friendly image drives sales – but in the case of Puma there is strong evidence that the two do not need to be mutually exclusive.

The efforts of Zeitz and Puma did not ring hollow. At the helm of one of the world's largest tobacco companies, Philip Morris International (PMI), the chief executive André Calantzopoulos found it harder to inhabit the role of a Campaigner. The Greek-born boss was compact, intense, a little edgy – a corporate Marlboro man with a rasping tone improbably attempting to convince the world to give up smoking.

'I hope this genuine effort will be appreciated by society,' he said, introducing PMI's iQOS smokeless cigarette, which used 'heat not burn' technology that his company's research suggested released far fewer toxins than conventional smoking.[18]

This did not feel like purpose championed alongside profit. It was more likely an act of self-preservation from a firm that still sold 847 billion cigarettes in 2015, the year before this interview, and 707 billion in 2019. As its core business continued to decline, PMI was grasping for a future with a higher-margin, lower-tax product it hoped to convince the US Food and Drug Administration (FDA) should be marketed to consumers as safer than traditional cigarettes.

Credit to Calantzopoulos for trying. He was appointed chief operating officer when PMI split in 2008 from Altria, which owns Marlboro in the US, and then chief executive from 2013. Leading the debate ahead of other tobacco firms that were rushing to develop their own so-called next-generation products was clearly beyond his comfort zone. But only two decades after Big Tobacco conceded that smoking caused lung cancer and emphysema and settled legal claims at great cost, it was a barely believable Damascene conversion, first of all by the company and then by its leader who had been selling cigarettes since he joined the business in 1985.

PMI and Calantzopoulos did not give up. An advertising campaign, entitled Unsmoke, carried slogans such as: 'If you don't smoke, don't start. If you smoke, quit. If you don't quit, change.' From a personal perspective he conceded it would be nice to have a positive impact on global health. 'Being trashed constantly is not exactly the most pleasurable experience you can have,' he said.[19]

This controversial Campaigner succeeded. In July 2020, PMI won approval from the FDA to market iQOS as a modified risk tobacco product, the first electronic nicotine device to receive such authorization. 'The FDA's decision is a historic public health milestone,' Calantzopoulos said. 'Many of the tens of millions of American men and women who smoke today will quit – but many won't. The FDA determined that scientific studies have shown that switching completely from conventional cigarettes to iQOS reduces exposure to harmful or potentially harmful chemicals.'[20]

Sense of mission

When Ajay Banga began hunting for his first job at the age of 21, he had only two requirements. The Delhi University economics graduate wanted to find a company that was global. And it also had to be good. Nestlé, the food and drink giant, fitted the bill.

Every leader's career is informed by their early experiences. The Lovers succeed in forging a career out of what they enjoy best. The Campaigners go one better by carrying a mission to drive change with them into the boardroom.

Banga's drive for diversity in business and his global outlook were helped by his upbringing in India, a religious and cultural melting pot he travelled around as his father, a senior army officer, moved bases. Goodness came from Sikhism and the faith's first leader, Guru Nanak, who spent the money his trader father had given him to set up a business feeding the hungry at the roadside. Financial inclusion was the natural angle for Mastercard to contribute towards the drive for greater social inclusion, which is 'not just what you look like or where you came from, it is about respecting you for who you are,' Banga said.

Winnie Byanyima, for many years the executive director of Oxfam International, can draw a direct line from her early experiences to the executive she became. Byanyima got her campaigning zeal from her parents. Living under Idi Amin's brutal Ugandan regime, her father was a local politician who was in and out of jail for refusing to switch allegiance to the ruling party. Her mother was a women's rights activist.

The opposed or oppressed – those whose land had been taken or whose rights had been denied – turned up at the childhood home she shared with five siblings. Acting as a magnet in this way meant life could be tough but Byanyima insisted it was character forming. 'It was a joyous time, it shaped me,' she said in 2015. 'I grew up really being able to stand up to authority.'[21]

Byanyima fled to Britain at the age of 17 and in 2013 became the first African to run an international development agency. Oxfam International is a confederation of 17 national organizations, active in 96 countries, with programmes in healthcare and education and numerous equality campaigns. In late 2019, she moved on to lead the joint United Nations programme on HIV and AIDS (UNAIDS) designed to coordinate global action for dealing with the disease.

Dame Helena Morrissey tackled similar injustices from the top down. This Campaigner wasn't looking for a cause but it sprang out at her in the normal cut and thrust of working life. Her 30% Club was conceived in November 2010 after a lunch for business leaders at the London headquarters of investment bank Goldman Sachs on Fleet Street, the former heart of the newspaper industry.

When talk turned to how women could break the glass ceiling in the City with little offered by way of a solution – as usual – Morrissey, the chief executive of funds firm Newton Investment Management, resolved not to let the next gathering that she was hosting in a few weeks' time become just another talking shop. She began contacting FTSE 100 chairmen, asking them to commit to having 30 per cent female representation on their boards by 2015 – a considerable lift from the 12.5 per cent rate at that time.

It was a very easy fit. The glass ceiling was something Morrissey had experienced during her City career. After joining the blue-blooded investment firm Schroders from Cambridge, she became the sole woman in a 16-person team of bond traders. At the age of 25, soon after returning from maternity leave after having her first child, Morrissey was passed over for promotion and decided to look around for other career opportunities. That took her to Newton where, ironically, a streak of promotions began in 1995 when her senior trading partner left to have a child of her own.

Her 30% Club ran alongside a UK government diversity campaign which had a slightly softer target. Suddenly everyone was on the bandwagon, but Morrissey – polite, firm, determined – stood out. Sat atop Newton's billions, she could credibly argue that balanced boards meant better businesses. As a mother of nine, she somehow wore lightly the pull of home life that had compromised the careers of so many working women. The club expanded to the United States in June 2014 with a goal of achieving 30 per cent female directors on S&P100 boards by 2020.

'I think it's one of those things that has a groundswell growing around what are the characteristics of a successful company in the future,' Morrissey said in a 2012 interview. 'It could make a big difference to the pace of change because company chairmen don't like to be hassled by investors.'[22]

Despite a strong sense of mission, it was only in September 2018, three years late, that FTSE 100 companies collectively hit the target conceived almost eight years earlier. The next goal was for boards of FTSE 350 companies – including the 250 next-largest firms outside the FTSE 100 – to feature 30 per cent women directors by the end of 2020. That was achieved ahead of time, in September 2019.

The collective effort kicked off by Morrissey that embraced investors, headhunters, chairmen and directors was a victory in correcting a very visible injustice. What was striking was the sense that hitting 30 per cent was a Pyrrhic victory because of the campaign's knock-on effect. It probably inspired more future or current women chief executives to 'go plural' sooner, that is switching from one full-time role to a portfolio of several part-time, non-executive posts. While a welcome campaign, it is likely to have depleted an already limited resource of female leaders. And campaigning for one form of diversity might have hogged the headlines and succeeded at the expense of making progress in other areas.

Undeterred, Morrissey has carried on campaigning, changing tack based on what she learnt last time. Her next cause, the Diversity Project, launched in 2016, pressed for a more inclusive culture in the savings and investment industry. It was framed as a much deeper dive into one City sector, looking at ways to improve diversity in all its forms – BAME, disability, gender, neurodiversity – in 50 firms that signed up. There were no concrete numerical targets to distract from effecting real change. 'It's time for the investment and savings industries to seek diversity in its broadest sense to ensure the industry has the cognitive and experiential diversity needed to be modern, to represent society and to make effective decisions,' Morrissey said at the launch.[23]

Conclusion

There was a time it appeared counterintuitive for businesses and their leaders to adopt a cause other than maximizing profit for shareholders. That time has passed.

In fact, even though committing to a parallel mission raises the risk profile of a role – something that canny leaders calculate is best lowered wherever possible – to fail to champion something that benefits society at large is an even greater risk. So great are the demands today for the widest possible stakeholder engagement that every corporate leader must be some part Campaigner if they are to prosper.

Not every leader is up to the challenge. Being an effective Campaigner is a test of how they put their platform to good use. It also tests how well they know their customers, staff, suppliers and investors. What they choose to champion has to be credible if minds must be changed to set off down a particular path. It must be broad enough for all staff to contribute and swell with pride, but narrowly aligned with the business itself. The cause must have attainable targets to keep everyone interested. It must not be a cynical attempt to boost sales – or look like one.

All of this demonstrates why Campaigners' personalities are so important. Causes can be very personal, even if they embrace an entire corporation. The individual must believe in what they are doing. It is why Campaigners are often one part Alpha, one part Lover – combining great force of will with great passion.

Returning briefly to Dame Helena Morrissey and Winnie Byanyima: both are Campaigners with much in common, eager to right wrongs that they have encountered personally and professionally. Where they differ is that one campaigns alongside a profit imperative while the other fundraises to achieve her goals. The rise of profit with purpose has mirrored purpose with profit – in other words charities acting much more commercially to achieve their aims.

It blurs the distinction between leadership qualities required in corporate and charitable settings. Consider that Oxfam International counted revenues in excess of €1 billion in the last financial year – from government grants, fundraising and retail income. Its leader must pitch for client support and make a margin before they can pursue their aims.

'We're not a charity' used to be a putdown for those accused of not acting in a sufficiently business-like way. Now business leaders should be inspired by charity bosses with great clarity of purpose who inspire passion in a largely volunteer workforce, keep a tight rein on costs and forge partnerships to maximize their impact. For their part, charity leaders, for whom trust is paramount, can learn from the discipline and good governance that corporate life demands.

Both brands of Campaigner might also consider the next chapter, where the smooth and supple Diplomats strive to keep a whole manner of stakeholders happy in profit and non-profit settings. They are stewards as much as leaders.

CAMPAIGNERS IN BRIEF

Strengths: Purpose, bravery, inspiring unity, righting wrongs, risk-taking.

Weaknesses: Possibly conflicted interests and strategic imbalance.

Suitability: Leading big brands, and big employers – the companies of scale that can make a difference. But even leaders of small firms should try.

Where you will find them: Increasingly everywhere. Profit with purpose is becoming engrained in corporate life.

Endnotes

This chapter: original Ajay Banga interview

1 The World Bank: The Global Findex Database 2017. https://globalfindex.worldbank.org/ (archived at https://perma.cc/33AY-7D56)

2 Federal Deposit Insurance Corporation (2017) FDIC National Survey of Unbanked and Underbanked Households. https://www.fdic.gov/householdsurvey/2017/2017report.pdf (archived at https://perma.cc/JXK3-E9QP)

3 YouTube (2019) Ajay Banga – President and CEO, Mastercard. https://www.youtube.com/watch?v=BhXKqjNEcFg&t=754s (archived at https://perma.cc/TE55-GAFV)

4 Unilever (2010) Unilever Sustainable Living Plan. https://www.unilever.com/Images/unilever-sustainable-living-plan_tcm244-409855_en.pdf (archived at https://perma.cc/LE8Q-ZRWV)

5 Ashton, J (2013) Stop me and buy one, says the Unilever ice cream man mixing new flavours of capitalism, *Evening Standard*, 19 July. https://www.standard.co.uk/business/markets/stop-me-and-buy-one-says-the-unilever-ice-cream-man-mixing-new-flavours-of-capitalism-8720071.html (archived at https://perma.cc/EN3G-65CS)

6 Unilever (2015) Mobilising Collective Action. https://www.unilever.com/Images/uslp-mobilising-collective-action-summary-of-progress-2015_tcm244-424809_en.pdf (archived at https://perma.cc/F8ZA-2YWB)

7 Financial Times (2016) Can Unilever's Paul Polman change the way we do business? 28 September. https://www.ft.com/content/e6696b4a-8505-11e6-8897-2359a58ac7a5 (archived at https://perma.cc/9JLK-ZKAF)

8 Unilever (2020) Unilever celebrates 10 years of the Sustainable Living Plan [Press Release] 6 May. https://www.unilever.com/news/press-releases/2020/unilever-celebrates-10-years-of-the-sustainable-living-plan.html#:~:text=London%2FRotterdam%20%2D%20Unilever%20today%20celebrated,its%20tenth%20and%20final%20year.&text=Speaking%20at%20a%20global%20virtual,game%2Dchanger%20for%20our%20business (archived at https://perma.cc/6XKR-QGDJ)

9   Patagonia (2020) Patagonia CEO Rose Marcario stepping down [Press Release] 10 June. http://www.patagoniaworks.com/press/2020/6/10/patagonia-ceo-rose-marcario-stepping-down (archived at https://perma.cc/NDB2-AFLA)

10 Beer, J (2018) Patagonia is in business to save our home planet, *Fast Company*, 13 December. https://www.fastcompany.com/90280950/exclusive-patagonia-is-in-business-to-save-our-home-planet?sf204319047=1 (archived at https://perma.cc/C7VS-5K8W)

11 Toms (nd) About Toms. https://www.toms.com/uk/about-toms.html (archived at https://perma.cc/62YW-NHNZ)

12 Roumeliotis, G (2019) Exclusive: TOMS Shoes creditors to take over the company, *Reuters*, 27 December. https://www.reuters.com/article/us-tomsshoes-m-a-creditors-exclusive/exclusive-toms-shoes-creditors-to-take-over-the-company-idUSKBN1YV1PT#:~:text=(Reuters)%20%2D%20TOMS%20Shoes%20LLC's,people%20familiar%20with%20the%20matter.&text=The%20group%20of%20creditors%2C%20led,Jefferies%20Financial%20Group%20Inc%20(JEF (archived at https://perma.cc/TN4U-6D63)

13 Puma (nd) Puma's EP&L. https://about.puma.com/en/sustainability/environment/measuring_environmental_footprint (archived at https://perma.cc/DZ75-ZZJG)

14 Ashton, J (2015) Jochen Zeitz: The businessman who uses his millions to change opinions on climate change, *Independent*, 5 April. https://www.independent.co.uk/environment/climate-change/jochen-zeitz-the-businessman-who-uses-his-millions-to-change-opinions-on-climate-change-10157482.html (archived at https://perma.cc/Q446-C8B9)

15 McFall-Johnsen, M (2020) These facts show how unsustainable the fashion industry is, *World Economic Forum*, 31 January. https://www.weforum.org/agenda/2020/01/fashion-industry-carbon-unsustainable-environment-pollution (archived at https://perma.cc/V4ZD-DD2R)

16 Ashton, J (2015) Jochen Zeitz: The businessman who uses his millions to change opinions on climate change, *Independent*, 5 April. https://www.independent.co.uk/environment/climate-change/jochen-zeitz-the-businessman-who-uses-his-millions-to-change-opinions-on-climate-change-10157482.html (archived at https://perma.cc/5JHY-X27W)

17   Puma (nd) Puma's EP&L. https://about.puma.com/en/sustainability/
     environment/measuring_environmental_footprint (archived at https://
     perma.cc/5VN8-Q5FT)

18   Ashton, J (2016) One day I hope we won't sell cigarettes, says
     Marlboro boss, *The Sunday Times*, October 23. https://www.thetimes.
     co.uk/article/one-day-i-hope-we-wont-sell-cigarettes-says-marlboro-
     boss-zfclkx5dt (archived at https://perma.cc/D3CE-ACW9)

19   Ibid.

20   Philip Morris International (2020) The U.S. FDA authorizes PMI's IQOS as
     a modified risk tobacco product, 7 July. https://www.pmi.com/media-center/
     news/u.s.-fda-authorizes-pmi-s-iqos-as-a-modified-risk-tobacco-product
     (archived at https://perma.cc/58XV-FVA9)

21   Ashton, J (2015) Winnie Byanyima interview: 'We don't think charity is
     the way to resolve global inequality' says Oxfam International Boss,
     Independent, 25 January. https://www.independent.co.uk/news/world/
     politics/winnie-byanyima-interview-we-dont-think-charity-is-the-way-
     to-resolve-global-inequality-says-oxfam-10001576.html (archived at
     https://perma.cc/FQ5F-8DZW)

22   Ashton, J (2012) Nine children, a £46bn investment firm and one
     broken washing machine, *Evening Standard*, 24 February

23   Diversity Project (2016) Industry unites to solve diversity levels 'once
     and for all', 20 October. https://diversityproject.com/2016-10-20/
     industry-unites-solve-diversity-levels-once-and-all (archived at https://
     perma.cc/92HV-CGAC)

CHAPTER EIGHT

Diplomats

A vocal majority

Across the bridge over the stream that separates the car park from the coffee shop, children shrieked with merriment as they played on a row of brightly coloured puzzles themed around flora and fauna. On a sunny midweek, midsummer's afternoon, here was England at play: tea, cake, a well-stocked garden centre and, through a cobbled archway, a glorious green pocket of suburban London.

Welcome to Morden Hall Park, a world away from the tatty town centre of Morden that lies at the southern tip of the Northern Line on London's underground network and a little too far for most Wimbledon locals to claim as their own. It is a site that has fulfilled many roles in its time. Once a deer park, a location for 1940s film star parties and home to a snuff mill, now all that roams its grounds are families looking for the best spot for a picnic or some carefree frisbee throwing.

The cream-coloured 18th-century hall at the park's heart has gone through its fair share of reinvention too, as a boys' school, a military convalescence home and, today, a wedding venue. After 75 years in the ownership of one family, on the death of the head of the household the core of the estate was transferred to the National Trust, the English, Welsh and Northern Irish conservation organization. The charity took over direct management in 1980, as it has done with numerous notable properties where death duties or running costs have proved overwhelming for long-term stewards.

If the National Trust was a company, then wandering around Morden Hall Park would be the equivalent of a factory visit. But this organization is far more than a corporation with the generation of sustainable financial returns at its heart. The keeper of the UK's national treasures – including Giant's Causeway in Northern Ireland, Fountains Abbey in North Yorkshire, a plentiful supply of stately homes and 780 miles of gorgeous coastline – touches many more lives than the average public limited company.

Such range presents great challenge and opportunity for its director-general. Until March 2018 that role was held by Dame Helen Ghosh, a formal but friendly former senior civil servant. On this particular trip to Morden Hall Park, she pinned a name badge to her jacket and stuck her head inside the garden centre to check on trading. Then it was off to the newly rebuilt stable yard, where tea and cake were waiting.

If Alphas are created by force of will or competitive relentlessness and Campaigners seize their chance and their platform to make a difference, the Diplomat provides a gentler form of leadership. Often they are a product of their surroundings, which can act as part comfort blanket, part constraint. More than any other leader type, they are likely to have impressed their peers to get where they are because Diplomats are often born from democracy, public servants in a private corporate setting promising to act on their manifesto promises.

But there is a trade-off that they risk ruling by consensus. The Diplomat must present the acceptable face of an organization while managing through the bureaucracy of diverse stakeholder voices. These contributors could own a partnership stake in the company – such as a City law or accounting firm – or just think they do.

Chief executives of companies that contain high numbers of knowledge workers reason the top-down approach to leadership is not appropriate for them. Instead they need to listen to ideas that bubble upwards. But despite the flow of honest talk, at organizations such as the National Trust, tradition unashamedly trumps transformation. A delicate leadership style is called for; a Diplomat at the helm who can take people with them can be no less effective than a leader who seeks to dominate with their thoughts and actions.

At a time when many organizations are battling dwindling interest, the National Trust counts 5.6 million members, making it the UK's largest membership organization. A recruitment drive, targeted at bringing in a younger demographic, meant that its fifth million was signed up in little more than six years up to 2017. By comparison, its first million took 86 years to gather. The organization was set up in 1895 by three impassioned Victorians, including the social reformer Octavia Hill, who wanted to preserve outdoor spaces.

Compare its popularity with the 3.2 million members of the Automobile Association who subscribe just in case they break down at the side of the road. Or the 191,000 who swear allegiance as members of the UK's ruling Conservative party – or the thinning band that go to church every Sunday morning.

The Trust is charged with preserving the fabric of the nation through its history, and with that responsibility comes a kaleidoscope of stakeholders. There are the founding families once responsible for historic buildings, local interest groups, town councils, wildlife clubs, 14,000 permanent and seasonal staff and 65,000 volunteers. Such a sprawl is reflected by the National Trust's governance structure that includes a 36-person council – half of whom are elected by the membership – acting as a check on the 12-person board of trustees. And then there is the national conscious, perhaps represented through the pages of the *Daily Mail* or *The Guardian* newspapers, making clear how they think heritage should be handled. The challenge is to bring them all together.

Often the person to do that has been a conservationist or similar but Dame Helen was someone steeped in diplomacy. She spent 33 years in the UK government's civil service, the politically impartial workforce at the heart of the state that implacably gets stuff done. Civil servants were satirized as wily Sir Humphrey in the television programme *Yes, Minister*, the situation comedy that was a favourite of British Prime Minister Margaret Thatcher.

Today, at a time of seemingly endless political turmoil, they are the corporate memory when so many ministers have come and gone. Brexit piled more pressure on them to remain rigidly independent but also keep the wheels of government turning, rather than become politicized like their American opposite numbers. The star of another BBC comedy, foul-mouthed spin doctor Malcolm Tucker in *The Thick of It*, filed the National Trust under the letter N in his 'little file of things I really don't give a f*** about'.[1] He was in a minority.

During her six-year reign, at times it felt as though everything Dame Helen did attracted criticism, such as praising wind turbines for their beauty, raising admission prices for older people, paying top dollar for Lake District farmland, weighing into the debate over climate change and supposedly dumbing down exhibition spaces by putting fewer artefacts on show or scattering cushions on the floor of grand houses so people could lounge about soaking up the hallowed surroundings.

Some of these were minor gripes but Dame Helen made it clear she was undeterred. She explained that her role was not purely about preserving things in aspic. 'Conservation is about managing the process of change, not keeping things exactly as they are,' she said.[2] All the same, it was a role that demanded consensus and that was sometimes hard to achieve despite a diplomatic pedigree earned building consensus across the government machine.

'As someone who is very rational, learning that emotional intelligence is just as important as logical argument, particularly when you are leading change, was a hard lesson,' Dame Helen said in another interview in 2015.[3]

It was ironic that criticism came as the National Trust negotiated the tyranny of choice granted by its sharply improved finances. Just like the changing role of Morden Hall Park over the years, its parent organization had changed tack too. It was a giant oil tanker that needed turning slowly, with annual income of £634 million in the year to February 2019. On Dame Helen's watch, that meant deciding how to spend £100 million a year on refurbishment or the National Trust's newer mission of acquiring and maintaining coastland and farmland.

Ultimately, those strategic decisions have to be taken by someone, regardless of their divisiveness. Going back over her career, Dame Helen painted herself as an honest broker thrown complicated, organizational challenges, such as regenerating the dilapidated east London, introducing a new scheme of tax credits and merging two tax authorities, the Inland Revenue and Customs & Excise. She rose to become Permanent Secretary at the Home Office and emphasized her collaborative skills. 'One thing you can trace through all of my professional life is the phrase: it's not a competition,' she said.[4] Dame Helen departed the National Trust in 2018 to become master of Balliol College at Oxford University.

It doesn't matter whether Diplomats succeed by collaborating or negotiating compromise – as long as appealing to the lowest common denominator does not become a recipe for disaster. The National Trust needed someone to listen, then act carefully. It is an example of an organization that heavily influences the type of leader it requires.

There is a school of thought that suggests being 'in charge' is an outdated concept, that success through inclusiveness is a modern antidote to the Alpha style of command and control. But good leadership cannot be defined by a lack of it. A leader should not have to radically moderate their behaviour to fit in with a stakeholder-led organization. Many Diplomats have no problem fitting in because they have been chosen straight from the pool of people they lead.

White-collar armies

So much changed in a handful of years in the City of London. Oddly-shaped skyscrapers sprouted across the skyline, a sign of exuberance and international wealth. Luxury boutiques were strung along Threadneedle Street and Cornhill, with posh grocer Fortnum & Mason colonizing one of the original hubs of commerce, the Royal Exchange, in 2018.

Less boisterous, more professional: the trading at the heart of Square Mile has seen open outcry go largely quiet and in its place is the low hum of mainframe computers, algorithms and indexation quietly calculated. The district has fanned out across London, with City firms heading east to Canary Wharf and as far as Stratford in the shadow of the Olympic stadium. It has spread south to More London Place, where lawyers and accountants share the riverside with the glass orb of City Hall, for now the Mayor of London's headquarters.

The banks that lived a little in the era of loose lending and looser morals have been constrained by new regulation and fresh leaders' promises. Technology has infiltrated the City, through new entrants challenging the hegemony of long-established lenders and insurers and start-up firms moving into Broadgate Circle, once a concrete temple of old money. The importance of good governance, risk controls, workplace equality and diversity have all risen in stature – although in all of these areas there is more work to be done.

Yet under the surface of this fast-moving, fiercely competitive, glossy, global, high-tech City, much has stayed the same. Namely the coterie of lawyers, accountants and consultants that populates London, the white-collar army that patrols the City on the lookout for clients and commission. They might be performing different tasks these days, using less paper, more smartphones, artificial intelligence and digital nous, but the core cradle-to-grave corporate advisory services – fundraising, deals, assurance, compliance, strategy and restructuring – are little changed.

So too is the structure of most of these firms. Not for them striking it rich like the brokers and merchant banks that sold out when the Big Bang tore down ownership restrictions for overseas firms in London in 1986. The bean counters and legal eagles have been quietly making hay ever since, maintaining partnership models that mean everyone – or at least a certain cadre of colleague – divides the spoils every year.

These firms have no shareholders to report to, no shares publicly listed that offer a running commentary on their prospects day after day. Instead, colleagues are responsible to each other, to their clients and to their future, which guides how much they invest back into the firm every year to keep pace with the competition. The central irony is that these are safety-first firms, even if outwardly they exude change and sometimes tell their clients to throw everything up in the air and start again. Their conservative heart aims to protect their franchise above all else.

The leadership of these firms, which include the Big Four accountants Deloitte, PWC, EY and KPMG, Magic Circle law firms Linklaters, Freshfields, Allen & Overy, Clifford Chance and Slaughter and May, and a smattering of consultants, is as carefully chosen as their product offering and pricing policy. Typically the front man – and it is still rarely a woman – is a safe choice, someone immensely trusted, long-serving, energetic, smart, presentable and perhaps ever so slightly bland. When things go wrong, they are the leader to put their head sufficiently above the parapet, smooth over the cracks and emote appropriately. They rarely speak out of turn. With hundreds of well-paid partners sat on their shoulder, they are a class of Diplomat all of their own.

David Sproul had the trust of his colleagues in spades because his role in the creation of the modern Deloitte was part of the firm's folklore. His previous firm Arthur Andersen was heading for collapse after its American practice became caught up in the implosion of Enron, the US energy trader that in 2001 was found to have carried out a vast accounting fraud.

As the UK firm's chief operating officer, Sproul was sent to New York in April 2002 to negotiate its sale to rival firm Deloitte & Touche. For hundreds of his fellow partners, whose wealth was tied up in Andersen, everything rode on his ability to get the job done. It took longer than Sproul thought – a bag packed for three days away was eked out for two weeks – but the deal was eventually sealed. A decade later, he was rewarded by being elected senior partner and chief executive of the enlarged firm, taking over the helm in 2011.

Deloitte has grown fast. During Sproul's eight-year term which ran to 2019, staff numbers rose by more than half to 19,000 at its combined UK and Swiss partnership, including 700 equity partners. Revenues just about doubled to £4 billion.

Not so long ago, Deloitte and its peer group preferred to operate discreetly in the slipstream of companies for which they worked. With intense scrutiny of the sector's output, especially over offshore tax advice and in the audit field after a series of high-profile failures, that is no longer possible. These Diplomats have had to step up and nurture their firms' profile – and to some extent their own.

In considering his legacy, Sproul – brisk, friendly, smooth, direct – pointed out two achievements in particular: the improved way in which Deloitte treated its people, including recruiting and training, and how the firm had globalized to work for clients across borders. Increased external demands had been matched by what colleagues expected of him internally.

'I spend far more time now talking to our people about who we are and what we stand for, what our values mean,' said Sproul, who went on staff charity cycle rides and took a third-floor office nearer the action compared to his predecessor's upstairs suite. 'We are not trying to make moral decisions for every one of our employees... They want to be connected to what we stand for in a way that perhaps wasn't as important 10 years ago.'[5]

Observers might say it sounds the same as it ever was. Sproul had to navigate contrasting views, including striking a balance between investing in the firm versus distributing profits to partners. He described how that broad ownership was a check on his leadership but also granted him a licence to operate on colleagues' behalf.

'There is something that really ensures that you don't ignore the interests of the owners but equally they expect you to make the right decisions,' he added. 'I have never found it difficult to convince the partners that we need to invest more because investing is about returns in the future which everyone benefits from.'

It is a similar story at PwC, Deloitte's closest rival whose combined UK and Middle Eastern partnership revenues reached £4.2 billion in the year to June 2019. Kevin Ellis, the UK senior partner and chairman since 2016, had many external factors to occupy him but was intent on doing a better job when talking internally to 24,000 staff including 900 UK partners.

'When I started out in the first year right after the (Brexit) referendum, business was tough and I thought we were getting on with it well and I was communicating well. At the end of the year, I realized that no one was listening,' Ellis said.

'People get caught in their own worlds... Everyone has got to know their role in the organization and how they fit into the strategy... My takeaway is whatever I think I am communicating well, times it by about ten.'[6]

These recurring challenges explain why partnership can opt for a recurring type of leader – a calming force with good communication skills. Sometimes their backgrounds are an unerring match. Just like his PwC predecessor, Sir Ian Powell, Ellis was a company lifer who studied in the English Midlands and elected to pursue corporate restructuring as his specialism and ultimate path to the top. Both of them even have four children.

Diplomats such as Sproul and Ellis have to tread a fine line. The hundreds of partners in each firm own a share and have their own view of what their firm should be. Auditors think audit is the most important division, and it traditionally has been, because of its umbilical link to blue-chip clients. Of course, consultants favour consulting, whether that is offering strategic advice or running major IT projects. It is fast-growing with fewer regulatory constraints. Bridging the divide within one company is diplomacy at work, especially as regulators look at prising the two sides apart to increase competition in the sector. If Diplomats can stay connected on all sides, their brand of gentle persuasion and mediation is highly effective at keeping business ticking over.

As the senior partner of Slaughter and May, Christopher Saul was keen to explain just how democratic the legendary City law firm was. In a legal industry that has raced to consolidate and plant flags across the world, Slaughters, founded by two young solicitors in 1889, might have become an anachronism. In fact it has remained a singular prospect.

Embedded in the City along with historic banking names such as Schroders, Rothschild and Barings, the firm also plugged into the 1980s Thatcher government when big-ticket privatizations were being planned. These days, the unique senior counsel it offers – just as the blue-blooded stockbroker Cazenove once did to a slew of FTSE 100 firms in corporate broking – means it has continued to prosper.

And, because it runs just one main office – a stylish fortress tucked away on Ropemaker Street close to Moorgate station – it can turn over much less than its Magic Circle rivals and still pay partners significantly more. However, it is too discreet to talk numbers.

Saul, who retired in 2016, was like a corporate maître d': dapper, unfailingly polite, conspiratorial without giving anything away, his City contacts book more extensive than any of the wine lists in the capital's best restaurants. Visitors to his office, where model cars adorned his desk and bookshelves, could be forgiven for wanting to slot a £20 note into his jacket pocket as they departed.

His description of Slaughters was more members' club than international law firm, with monthly board meetings plus partner gatherings once a quarter to make up new partners and chew over major decisions. The dining room also played host to the firm-wide conversation. Partners each had a pigeon hole for their napkin. Saul explained: 'We are refreshing the bond every day.'[7]

It was easy to see how he was chosen to lead. Saul described his job as to 'celebrate and support the success of the firm, to be a figurehead, put things on the agenda and say, hey everybody, what do you think?' Softly, softly. Slaughters had no need for a table-thumper leading its subtle public profile. Save the tricky conversations for behind closed doors.

A key speech

These Diplomats have longevity in common. Before being chosen for the top job, David Sproul had notched up 27 years at Deloitte, Kevin Ellis 32 years at PwC and Chris Saul 31 years at Slaughters. So important is culture and continuity to this sector that firms will never install an outsider such as a Fixer or a Seller at the helm.

Sir Philip Dilley had spent 33 years at Arup before being appointed executive chairman from 2009 until 2014, selected by trustees to serve a maximum five-year term. The partnership model extends from accountants to engineers, through his firm, which has worked on famous structures including the Sydney Opera House, New York's Fulton Center, the National Aquatics Center in Beijing and the Øresund Bridge that connects Denmark and Sweden and had a bleak TV drama named after it.

'It is a place that gives you an awful lot of freedom with a bit of a safety net, as well as access to a fabulous knowledge base,' Sir Philip said as he explained why he had stayed so long.[8] That reasoning is not so different to other Diplomats. Just like most Lovers, they are one-firm men and women for whom it was simply too hard to leave. What sets Sir Philip apart from the rest of his cohort is the strong steer he was given from beyond the grave about how he should lead Arup.

On 9 July 1970, concerned as various original leaders began to retire that the firm's ethos might be lost, the eponymous founder Sir Ove Arup addressed colleagues at an event in the English city of Winchester. His 'key speech' covered topics such as quality of work, social usefulness and reasonable prosperity. It also described the principles of leadership and ownership he envisioned after putting his shares in the firm into trust along with fellow partners for the benefit of future employees.

More than 50 years on and following Sir Ove's death in 1988, it is a legacy that looms large over the firm and a text that every new joiner is still encouraged to read – even the part about good-looking secretaries, which has not aged well. For the Diplomat it resonates.

'In the Ove Arup Partnership we have all but eliminated ownership – the senior partners only act as owners during their tenure of office because someone has to, according to the laws of the country,' said Sir Ove, adding, 'It may be possible to devise a different and better arrangement than the one we have now – more "democratic", more fair. It may be possible to build in some defences against the leaders misbehaving and developing boss complexes and pomposity, and forgetting that they are just as much servants in a good cause as everybody else – only more so.'

Later in the speech, which Sir Ove confessed should have been one-third the length, he returned to the subject. 'I think it is unavoidable that "we" should mean different things in different contexts. Sometimes what is said is only relevant to the upper layers of management, sometimes it is meant to include everybody. What we must aim at is to make "we" include as many as possible as often as possible. To increase the number of those who have a contribution to make, however small, who agree wholeheartedly with our aims and want to throw in their lot with us. We might think about them as members of our community; the others, who come and go, might be called staff. Of course there can never be any clear line of demarcation, it is not a question of signing a form or bestowing a title, it is a matter of how each feels and what we feel about them. For it is a two-way business.

'But what binds our membership together must be loyalty to our aims. And only as long as the leaders of the firm are loyal to these can they expect and demand loyalty from the members.'[9]

So Sir Philip and his successors must be content to be first among equals, a representative kept in check by colleagues as much as charged to lead them. This subversion of the traditional role of leader doesn't sound much fun and yet it seems to work for the group. Arup's revenues increased by more than 50 per cent to £1.7 billion in the four years to 2019.

Alan Belfield, the chairman since 2019, is relaxed about reining in activities that stretch from rail infrastructure and energy schemes to developing a midwife leadership programme for hospitals to a drainage masterplan for flood-prone Shanghai. Shorn of external investors demanding focus or higher returns, Arup 'members' are extended plenty of choice about the work they take on. With a light-touch leadership, Belfield describes Arup's practices around the world as 'little villages' that 'might argue with one another' but always make up in the end.[10]

Getting chosen

In spring 2019, as he was preparing to step down after eight years in charge, Deloitte's David Sproul explained the firm's election process that offers every partner the chance to vote for who runs the firm. 'Despite being a global, modern organization there is one thing which is slightly archaic and that is the way we elect our leaders,' he conceded.[11] Sproul identified two prongs to his successful leadership campaign.

'You have to present the manifesto – this is what you are going to achieve in your chapter of this great firm – but you also have to win hearts and minds because in the end they are electing a leader, and people like to follow their leader.'

Candidates' pledges have much in common. They want to grow their organization, build client relationships and improve working conditions. There is a wide range of views to represent and the successful candidate is the one that can find common ground. Personality plays a crucial role. They must put themselves on show to win the trust of their peers.

Sproul added, 'When I first went to pitch I stood up in front of 700 partners and I spoke about my wife and daughters, who they were and what they thought about what I was doing... Half thought that was really helpful, half thought, why is he telling us this? It just shows the range of emotions in our organization. Some wanted total empathy, others were just not interested at all.'[12]

Rather than pitch formally to their peers, Chris Saul at Slaughters explained that his firm's selection process was formed around a series of cosy chats. If you want to be nominated 'you would somehow let it subtly be known', he said.[13] That leads to a secret ballot and then the corporate equivalent of some papal white smoke emerges, but the principle is the same. The boss owes his seat to those around him and is at once leader and grateful servant.

Not so, according to Kevin Ellis, who in 2020 was chosen unopposed for a second four-year term at PwC and felt empowered by the result. 'It does give you a right to lead and I think you have got to respect that,' he said. 'I know they (the partners) agree with the strategy I am following.'[14]

Nor does the idea of picking a safe candidate always ring true. When Richard Houston succeeded Sproul in 2019, he was the first UK leader in Deloitte's 175-year history with a consulting background. 'Is that frightening the horses? I was not what you would call a traditional candidate,' he said. 'I would say the most important thing about partner-based organizations is engagement and transparency.'

Checkout time

When most people in the UK think of a partnership company, they think of the John Lewis Partnership (JLP), home to the much-loved middle-class department store of the same name as well as supermarket chain Waitrose & Partners. In the cut-throat, hyper-competitive, zero-hours era, it has been held up as the epitome of what it is to be employee-friendly and customer caring – as well as the go-to place for luxury food and furnishings. Following the financial crash of 2008, government ministers quickly called for the creation of more firms that followed the model of John Lewis-style employee ownership, even spinning off a handful of such ventures from Whitehall themselves.

It was the retailer's founder, John Spedan Lewis, who left a unique inheritance for shop workers when he died in 1963. The group was put into a trust for employees – or 'partners' – who were entitled to a share of the profits every year. There is also a written constitution in place so what was termed an 'experiment in industrial democracy' could continue indefinitely.[15]

One example is the executive pay cap that limits the pay of the highest-paid partner to no more than 75 times the average basic pay of non-management partners, calculated on an hourly basis. Whereas elsewhere the gap between top and bottom widened, JLP was held up for championing fairness and as a pioneer in boosting worker productivity. Rivals might have sniped that it hamstrung the group from hiring the best talent, but it bred collegiate leaders instead. Just like Sir Ove Arup's speech, the remuneration rule and others meant the leadership path here had clear parameters. JLP can only ever be led by someone who buys into the inclusive nature of the company: in other words, a Diplomat.

That generosity of spirit, which also shows itself in pay and perks, breeds fierce loyalty. Lord (Mark) Price spent 34 years at JLP after joining as a graduate trainee in 1982 and starting out in the lighting department of John Lewis's Southampton store. He rose to become managing director of Waitrose. Since leaving in 2016 he has served as the UK's trade minister, written on the fairness agenda and set up the website Engaging Works that set out to help people get more from their careers.

Price is a staunch defender of the JLP model. 'There has never been a time when a form of inclusive capitalism is more important, frankly,' he said. 'I think rewarding the people in your business for the value they create is a very of-its-time idea.'[16]

The trouble was that for several years the John Lewis difference had not shown up in the numbers. In March 2020, the group disclosed a third straight decline in annual profits to £123 million and the bonus for its 80,000 workers was cut to just 2 per cent of salary, the lowest since 1953. Worse was to come in July, when John Lewis disclosed that eight of its 50 department stores would close after the Covid-19 pandemic accelerated the switch to shopping online.

Retail is intensely competitive even without a global health emergency, but it is impossible not to think the group's production line of Diplomats has been found wanting in any case. In early 2020, the departing chairman Sir Charlie Mayfield left the business after 20 years with a foggy proposal to crash together the management structure of John Lewis department stores and the Waitrose supermarket side that led to the exit of dozens of senior staffers. Included in the exodus were the managing directors of Waitrose and John Lewis, Rob Collins and Paula Nickolds, graduate trainees from 1993 and 1994 respectively. The overwhelming feeling was that the largely homegrown leadership was best suited to gentler times.

'The instinct is that just doing a bit more of what you did before a bit better will be all right on the night,' Sir Charlie said in a 2019 interview.[17] 'It might be for a year or two, but it won't be long term. Our strategy needs to be much more bold.' This is the Achilles heel of Diplomats. Long-serving insiders who live and breathe the culture are often not the leaders to make radical change when it is demanded.

Succeeding Sir Charlie was Dame Sharon White, a newcomer in the Diplomat mould with little retail experience. She proved to be a safe pair of hands leading Ofcom, the UK media regulator, but before that she blazed a trail through the civil service from 1989 onwards, including stints at the Department for International Development, Ministry of Justice and Department for Work and Pensions.

At the Treasury, rising to Second Permanent Secretary, she oversaw a review of the department's response to the financial crisis and implemented spending cuts. She can be consensual, yes, but it remains to be seen whether Dame Sharon's decision making is deft enough to guarantee JLP a healthier future when a ruthless Fixer might have been a better fit.

Head of the flotilla

On a sunset cruise chugging up the River Thames, Robin Mortimer was relishing the opportunity to lead. He described ambitious plans to drive up cargo and passenger volumes in his role as chief executive of the Port of London Authority (PLA). Aboard one of the numerous pleasure boats that patrol London's central river artery every evening it was obvious this cruise was business, not pleasure.

The PLA acts as custodian of the tidal Thames, which runs 95 miles west to east from Teddington Lock in

Richmond upon Thames, to the North Sea. The organization has a key role in ensuring navigational safety, which means giant container ships, commuter boats and wildlife can all happily co-exist. It is also a more challenging role over the next decade as river cargo heads towards surpassing the peak volume achieved in 1964 and more of the capital's workers take to the river to travel to work. The reason for the cruise was to drum up interest in the PLA's new strategy, a 20-year vision to show that the Thames could grow its use and economic contribution to London.

Mortimer had a rising tide of revenue to put those plans into action. At £67 million in 2019, income was up almost a third in five years, with the majority coming from fees charged to cargo ships to cover river maintenance and pilotage. Nevertheless, the host of stakeholders he must manoeuvre between risks getting as crowded as his waterway. It is just as well this Diplomat has 20 years in the civil service working for several UK cabinet ministers under his belt. And, as an informal mentor, Mortimer leant on Dame Helen Ghosh to talk through making the transition from the corridors of Whitehall into a leadership role at the PLA in 2014.

While in the civil service, Mortimer's briefs included environment, water industry pricing and transforming the government-owned British Waterways into the Canal & River Trust, a charity that oversees 2,000 miles of canals and rivers in England and Wales. If he had stayed he would surely have become a Permanent Secretary, steering one of the large departments of government, but Mortimer wanted the autonomy that only a life outside could offer. 'More than anything, I would say that being outside government you have the ability to shape your destiny and shape the organization,' he said in 2019.[18]

Despite that hint of frustration, Mortimer also praised what he learnt and how it set him up to tackle big problems as the boss. Preparing a new PLA strategy was very much like preparing a government white paper – or policy document – by collecting opinions and reflecting on the best way forward. 'At its best I think the civil service is really good at bringing evidence to bear on a problem and trying to solve it,' he said. 'That disciplined, structured way of thinking is really great training.'[19]

These are skills that are bound up with leading. The ministers hold the reins of power in each department, but it isn't exactly how it feels inside the system, Mortimer claimed, adding: 'The civil service does a lot of leading on policy and the relationship with ministers is at its best a creative one where the civil servants are doing some of the thought leadership.'[20]

Conclusion

A great leadership skill is distilling the complex into the simple. It is something at which Diplomats must excel. They are at their best when a balance has to be struck, a path picked through the views of numerous stakeholders and a minefield of dissent.

They listen, they learn, they keep the ship steady. They are not out-and-out changemakers and may not move as fast as some in the cut-throat competitive world of business are required to do.

Diplomats should not be seen as weak leaders but they can suffer from being handed weak mandates. Jointly owned cannot mean jointly run. But there are numerous examples of success through working towards collaborative aims with a light-touch leadership. Consensus and commercial success are not mutually exclusive.

Close engagement with the workforce – and volunteer force – is crucial in the modern world. As more organizations attempt to be truly inclusive, Diplomats, the great communicators, have skills that crop up again in the ninth leadership type, Humans.

DIPLOMATS IN BRIEF

Strengths: Listening, evidence gathering, communication, finding consensus, evolution not revolution.

Weaknesses: Caution, holding onto tradition, perhaps in need of a stronger mandate to increase effectiveness.

Suitability: Partnership firms, organizations with broad stakeholder interests.

Where you will find them: Wherever they have been voted in or gravitated to the top of an organization.

Endnotes

This chapter: original Richard Houston interview

1   YouTube (2017) 'The Thick of It – Malcolm Tucker's list of things he doesn't give a f**k about. https://www.youtube.com/watch?v=22PR8ZNDAO8 (archived at https://perma.cc/7P5H-9SBM)

2   Ashton, J (2015) Dame Helen Ghosh: Ex Senior Home Office figure on using her skills to help the National Trust deal with climate change,

Independent, 12 July. https://www.independent.co.uk/news/uk/
home-news/dame-helen-ghosh-ex-senior-home-office-figure-on-using-
her-skills-to-help-the-national-trust-deal-10383704.html (archived at
https://perma.cc/D7N9-KK92)

3 Isaac, A (2015) Be confident, be bold: 10 tips from female charity leaders,
Independent, 7 March. https://www.theguardian.com/voluntary-sector-
network/2015/mar/07/10-tips-female-charity-leaders-international-womens-day
(archived at https://perma.cc/P857-NB9P)

4 Ashton, J (2015) Dame Helen Ghosh: Ex Senior Home Office figure on
using her skills to help the National Trust deal with climate change,
Independent, 12 July. https://www.independent.co.uk/news/uk/ home-news/
dame-helen-ghosh-ex-senior-home-office-figure-on-using-her-skills-to-help-
the-national-trust-deal-10383704.html (archived at https://perma.cc/
D7N9-KK92)

5 Ashton, J (2019) Leading with James Ashton Episode 1 – Deloitte and
Teenage Cancer Trust, *Apple Podcasts*, 29 April. https://podcasts.apple.
com/gb/podcast/episode-1-deloitte-and-teenage-cancer-trust/
id1460796936?i=1000436797958 (archived at https://perma.cc/
85UB-BJD9)

6 Ashton, J (2019) Leading with James Ashton S3 Episode 2 – PwC and
Great Ormond Street Hospital, *Apple Podcasts*, 13 April. https://
podcasts.apple.com/gb/podcast/s3-episode-2-pwc-and-great-ormond-
street-hospital/id1460796936?i=1000471311736 (archived at https://
perma.cc/DCX4-2B4A)

7 Ashton, J (2014) Chris Saul interview: Slaughter and May purrs like a
Porsche but that doesn't mean we're run by Buffy and Bertie,
Independent, 24 November. https://www.independent.co.uk/news/
people/profiles/chris-saul-interview-slaughter-and-may-purrs-like-a-
porsche-but-that-doesn-t-mean-we-re-run-by-buffy-9878727.html
(archived at https://perma.cc/8UM4-9HCZ)

8 Ashton, J (2012) Interview: Arup's Philip Dilley is bringing bold ideas
from the sketchpad to reality, *Evening Standard*, 2 March. https://www.
standard.co.uk/business/markets/interview-arups-philip-dilley-is-
bringing-bold-ideas-from-the-sketchpad-to-reality-7499177.html
(archived at https://perma.cc/9AJ2-8G8D)

9   Arup (nd) Ove Arup Key Speech. https://www.arup.com/perspectives/
     publications/speeches-and-lectures/section/ove-arup-key-speech
     (archived at https://perma.cc/Z28F-TUJC)

10 Ashton, J (2020) Answering the questions posed by Covid will be good
     for our business, *The Times*, 17 July. https://www.thetimes.co.uk/article/
     answering-the-questions-posed-by-covid-will-be-good-for-our-business-
     85cwsbg3j (archived at https://perma.cc/2X2F-679U)

11 Ashton, J (2019) Leading with James Ashton Episode 1 – Deloitte and
     Teenage Cancer Trust, *Apple Podcasts*, 29 April. https://podcasts.apple.
     com/gb/podcast/episode-1-deloitte-and-teenage-cancer-trust/
     id1460796936?i=1000436797958 (archived at https://perma.
     cc/85UB-BJD9)

12 Ibid.

13 Ashton, J (2014) Chris Saul interview: Slaughter and May purrs like a
     Porsche but that doesn't mean we're run by Buffy and Bertie,
     Independent, 24 November. https://www.independent.co.uk/news/
     people/profiles/chris-saul-interview-slaughter-and-may-purrs-like-a-
     porsche-but-that-doesn-t-mean-we-re-run-by-buffy-9878727.html
     (archived at https://perma.cc/8UM4-9HCZ)

14 Ashton, J (2019) Leading with James Ashton S3 Episode 2 – PwC and
     Great Ormond Street Hospital, *Apple Podcasts*, 13 April. https://
     podcasts.apple.com/gb/podcast/s3-episode-2-pwc-and-great-ormond-
     street-hospital/id1460796936?i=1000471311736 (archived at
     https://perma.cc/DCX4-2B4A)

15 John Lewis (2017) The Constitution of the John Lewis Partnership.
     https://www.johnlewispartnership.co.uk/content/dam/cws/pdfs/
     about-us/our-constitution/john-lewis-partnership-constitution.pdf
     (archived at https://perma.cc/6ZTB-BBXB)

16 Ashton, J (2018) Mark Price interview: Meet the 'Chubby Grocer'
     who wants his Engaging Works to be the John Lewis of social media
     (and insists he won't sell your data), *Mail on Sunday*, 11 November.
     https://www.thisismoney.co.uk/money/news/article-6375867/Mark-
     Price-interview-want-john-Lewis-social-media.html (archived at
     https://perma.cc/DK7Z-M58U)

17 Craven, N (2019) As his stores plunge into red, John Lewis chairman
     Sir Charlie Mayfield says: Yes, losses hurt but I'm getting retail giant fit
     for the Amazon age, *Mail on Sunday*, 14 September. https://www.

thisismoney.co.uk/money/experts/article-7464279/Sir-Charlie-Mayfield-Yes-losses-hurt-Im-getting-John-Lewis-fit-Amazon-age.html (archived at https://perma.cc/K4HZ-T8T6)

18 Ashton, J (2019) Robin Mortimer is not messing about when he says tide is turning for the Thames, *The Times*, 29 June. https://www.thetimes.co.uk/article/this-man-is-not-messing-about-when-he-says-tide-is-turning-for-the-thames-z5373wlq2 (archived at https://perma.cc/S7RQ-BBSH)

19 Ashton, J (2019) Leading with James Ashton Episode 5 – Royal Society and Port of London Authority, *Apple Podcasts*, 27 May. https://podcasts.apple.com/gb/podcast/episode-5-royal-society-and-port-of-london-authority/id1460796936?i=1000439680583 (archived at https://perma.cc/BWH4-A9JU)

20 Ibid.

CHAPTER NINE

Humans

A green dream

Under the gleaming chandeliers of the Festsaal, a sumptuous imperial stateroom in Vienna's sprawling Hofburg palace, they gathered to talk about managing for the long term. The venue could not have been more appropriate. From this base, Habsburg kings and emperors ruled the Holy Roman Empire for more than three centuries split into two stints.

The Austrian capital was also the home town of the celebrated management guru Peter Drucker, whose philosophy is celebrated annually at this conference, the Global Peter Drucker Forum. For three days every November, company strategists, consultants and hundreds of students of management come to hear academics and deep boardroom thinkers opine about the challenges of modern leadership and management. They cannot do so without delving into the past. After all, it was Drucker, who died in 2005, who insisted managers had a responsibility to the whole of society and not just their shareholders.

For this post-lunch session at 2018's event, one of the draws was Isabelle Kocher, the chief executive of Engie, the French energy giant once known more prosaically as Gaz de France (GDF) Suez. Kocher, elegant and impassioned, had emerged as a star, the first woman to run one of France's blue-chip CAC 40 companies. She was determined to leave her mark. Seated alongside her was Paul Polman, who had just flown in from New York after announcing his retirement from consumer goods giant Unilever the day before.

It was a symbolic baton passing. Here was Polman, the veteran Campaigner featured in Chapter 7 of this book, joking that he was looking for a job now because his wife would not put up with him at home. Far from indulging in her own retrospective, Kocher set out the rapid-fire progress made so far since she had taken the reins two-and-a-half years earlier. If successful, Engie would be transformed from the business she had worked for in some form for the last 16 years since 2002, when she joined the French water firm Suez which merged with GDF in 2008.

Kocher had set in motion the biggest shake-up of the former state-owned gas monopoly since the European Union decreed that its domestic market needed to be opened to competition by 2000 and it set off to acquire international power interests. Soon after taking the helm, she declared that the energy giant would sell 20 per cent of its assets – worth some €15 billion – as she reconfigured the corporation for a low-carbon future. Years before many fossil-fuel firms saw the light, out would go dirty coal and gas and most of the proceeds would be redeployed in wind, solar and hydropower generation and storage. She insisted society was driving her strategy, but that shareholders would welcome it too.

'By definition you are absolutely at the core of the problem,' Kocher said on the sidelines of the Drucker event, citing statistics that found the energy industry was responsible for 60 per cent of all carbon dioxide emissions. 'You have a choice: either continue like that and become more and more part of the problem, or you try to become part of the solution.'

It was a typically bold move from a modern type of leader. Deft, short-term actions mapped out with the long term in mind, all packaged and delivered with supreme confidence. Immediately, Kocher – who had had a long handover period since October 2014 when she was made up to deputy chief executive under chairman and chief executive Gérard Mestrallet – made the connection between the planet, profit and her people and used it to inform her strategy in a way that her predecessors had not.

They are more inclusive, more diverse, more digital, more experimental: the next generation of business leader wants to act fast not slow, be caring not careless, stick close to their workforce and put purpose ahead of profit. Picking the best of what has gone before them, they know they must justify their existence, often stripping back what leadership means altogether in a mission to please a wide spread of stakeholders. And conscious of the importance of communication, they want to be seen to be doing the right thing too. In fact, what they want more than anything else is to be Human.

The Humans are a leadership type far removed from the Masters of the Universe of boardrooms past. They are determined to emerge from their ivory tower and break down the walls that encircle their empire. They know that modern corporations are more porous than ever – thanks to social media and websites such as Glassdoor where employees review the companies they work for – but that shouldn't stop them running them to the best of their ability.

Their firms are carefully embedded in society, and as leaders they are embedded alongside colleagues who they view as a vital asset, not only an ideas resource, but an army of advocates. They are also acutely self-aware so as to deploy their time and their powers in the most effective way possible.

Kocher might have championed her corporate vision on stages such as at the Drucker event, but she regularly made clear she was not acting individually. 'I don't believe in leaders who have the wisdom alone to define (a strategy),' she said. 'The name of the game is to provoke the fact that everybody feels in charge of the emergence of this vision.'

Before taking the helm of Engie, she toured the company, speaking to many of its 155,000 staff, non-governmental organizations, politicians and tech companies to gauge their view on the future path it should take. Their input ran in parallel with an in-depth analysis designed to screen out Engie's activities that could not make the transition to a zero-carbon world. They would be quickly sold.

By April 2019, coal made up only 4 per cent of Engie's generating capacity, compared with 13 per cent at the end of 2015, after the disposal of the group's coal-fired power plants in the Netherlands and Germany was announced. In addition, Engie committed €12 billion to invest in cleaner energy solutions for corporates and local authorities, large-scale development of renewable energy, and the necessary adaptation of power and gas networks to the energy transition.

The staff consultation could have been dismissed as a publicity stunt if Kocher hadn't repeated it to define a 2030 vision for the company, encouraging colleagues not just to contribute their ideas but also to interview clients and contacts for their opinions. Determined to decentralize and lower the centre of gravity of the organization, she said, 'Sometimes people think that for a bigger organization it is more difficult to change than a small one. I see the point but having so many people… they are also part of society themselves. It is like you have thousands of centres and you can really leverage that.'

Her plan to be the first choice for clients, investors and staff was working – at least if the 60 per cent increase in résumés that Engie received was anything to go by. Kocher was convinced it was a virtuous circle: 'It is not an arbitrage between social responsibility and value creation. You cannot perform from an economic point of view if you don't align with what the client needs.'

Some further Drucker words of wisdom could almost have been written for Kocher. 'Your first and foremost job as a leader is to take charge of your own energy,' he wrote, 'and then help to orchestrate the energy of those around you.'[1]

Kocher did not get the chance to see her transformation through because on 6 February 2020 Engie's board terminated her chief executive mandate. On 24 February she tweeted: 'I leave @ENGIEgroup with absolute serenity and immense emotion.'

This Human had tried to keep all constituents happy while leading the transformation of a complicated international business. But she had been a casualty of boardroom infighting amid concern about the price achieved from some asset disposals and a disappointing stock performance versus that of peers. The French state, a 24 per cent shareholder that had backed an early 30 per cent cut in the dividend, was reported to be instrumental in the decision. In an interview soon after, Engie's chairman Jean-Pierre Clamadieu said that Kocher 'did not manage to demonstrate that she was the right person to deepen the group's transformation'.[2]

No one said it was going to be easy striving to find a new way of leading. And some might not be ready for those who are guided by flashes of inspiration. What is demanded regardless of the vision and the method is that tangible results follow closely on. Humans are fallible, sure, but they are not a byword for failure – more of a work in progress. In the next section, meet the leaders who think less means more in modern business.

Taking a sledgehammer

Zhang Ruimin's 1984 arrival at a failing electricals factory in Qingdao, a city in the Shangdong province south of

Beijing, has passed into corporate folklore. The council official was the latest in a line of managers who had come and gone in quick succession.

'My goal initially was just simply to enable the workers to be paid and to enable the company to run normally and then I would leave,' he said, reflecting on the posting in 2018.

Zhang took an immediate interest in the factory's quality control, which at that time in China was an alien concept. China had a system for classifying industrial products into first, second and third grade – or no grade at all – which made it acceptable to ship goods that were far from perfect. 'It was that kind of mindset that we wanted to eliminate. We also got letters from our customers claiming that some products were of a low quality.'

Zhang inspected a consignment of 400 refrigerators before they were shipped and found that 76 of them had problems. Eager to make a point, he obtained a sledge-hammer and called a staff meeting.

'We found out who was responsible for those defects and put the names of the workers on those refrigerators. Then we asked those people to smash those refrigerators themselves.

'Some workers cried. There were tears because people thought it was OK that if something was not first class it could be second class but I wanted to tell people that a defective product was just a waste. It was important to establish the mindset for total quality management, which is the Japanese way of managing.' To emphasize the point, he began linking pay to product quality.

Finding freedom

Zhang might have been a Fixer if it wasn't for the evolving way in which he has continued to run his company as chairman and chief executive. That failing factory was the kernel of a company that over more than three decades has been transformed into Haier, a home appliances giant whose washing machines, refrigerators, microwave ovens and air conditioners battle for consumers' attention with Whirlpool, Bosch, Miele, Hotpoint and others. And setting aside the sledgehammer – which today sits in a glass case in company headquarters – it is what Zhang did next that marks him out as a Human.

'I believe hierarchical companies will eventually die off, whereas networked organizations – which are self-organized, not organized by others – will sustain,' he declared on a trip to Vienna for his own appearance at the Global Peter Drucker Forum.

China might not be the first market that springs to mind for experimenting with hands-off leadership; its political masters are anything but. But Zhang, who has been garlanded with awards for his management think-ing, lives by the expression 'management without leader-ship'. It sounds like a way to absolve himself of blame if anything goes wrong but that isn't the idea. Speaking through a translator in a hotel meeting room packed with perhaps eight other people including a film crew making a recording of his European trip, he was courteous but inscrutable.

'My role is to build a platform and provide services so entrepreneurs can succeed faster,' he said. It sounds like he has drunk too much Kool-Aid but so far it appears to have worked. The parent company remains private but Haier's main listed unit, Haier Smart Home, whose shares trade in Shanghai and Frankfurt, reported a healthy 9 per cent increase in sales in 2019 to RMB201 billion, with profits rising almost 10 per cent to RMB8.2 billion thanks to growing demand for networked appliances, connected through the 'Internet of Things' (IOT). The group commands more than 10 per cent of the world home appliance market and has a retail presence in 160 countries and 122 manufacturing plants.

Zhang's model is to give staff great freedom. His entrepreneurs are 2,000 self-managed Haier teams that emerged when Zhang took a sledgehammer to the middle-management layer. These micro enterprises bid internally for customer orders and more than 200 of them have already attracted venture capital investment. Invoking Drucker, he added, 'In new ways of management we no longer need traditional leaders because everyone can be their own CEO.' Employees even decide how much they should be paid, based on how much value they have created for Haier.

Zhang claimed there were two reasons to reinvent an organization even if it seemed to be running well. He fights against so-called 'large enterprise disease', which he defines as 'when a company grows to a certain scale, becoming less responsive, and there are deeper and deeper conflicts in the organization and it is further and further away from the end-user'. Secondly, Zhang said that all organizations face a dual purpose, 'to run business as usual, especially as a large company, and secondly to innovate. It seems that no company can achieve these two goals at the same time; they seem to be conflicting with each other, and I wanted to address that.' His underlying theme is that corporate leaders are not as important as they once were.

Learning from others

Zhang's epiphany came as General Electric fell into difficulty. Haier and Zhang have a long history with the US industrial giant, whose troubles were covered in the Alphas chapter. Zhang had long idolized Jack Welch, the legendary leader of GE who built up the business over 20 years to 2001.

In 1992, Haier fell out with GE when the Chinese firm opted not to become the US firm's contract manufacturer for the region. It set Haier on an acquisitive path because Zhang knew Haier had to grow in sales and ideas if he was to stand toe-to-toe with global rivals. In 2016, Haier triumphantly acquired GE's electrical appliances arm for $5.6 billion – some 24 years after his firm might have been bought by them.

With their history, it was unsurprising that Zhang was dismissive of GE's 'super empire' which had switched leadership several times since Welch. The company had been running 'very much how the US was fighting its war against terror in 2013', he said. 'It had the greatest military power and technology but it still was not effective in fighting Sunni terrorists.' His own empire building had been discarded.

'Our goal used to be to build an empire. Then we realized empires will usually collapse and that is why we changed our goal. Instead of building a huge aircraft carrier we realized it was better to build a fleet of combat ships. To put it into one sentence we are changing the organization's goal from producing products to producing entrepreneurs.' In explaining what role the leader, or captain, plays in this set-up, Zhang had even more combative analogies.

'In traditional companies the captain designs the ship, whereas in our organization the captain designs the fleet or how the mechanism for which different ships in the fleet work and fight together flexibly,' he said. 'In World War II it seems the most effective strategy was not how big the warship was but how you can fight the enemy like a pack of wolves.'

China is often accused of taking the best ideas from around the world and making them their own, often with little regard for intellectual property. Haier has been more respectful. Zhang's method of leadership is magpie-like, taking the best of Japanese management, then US globalization and brand-building, to form his own way of thinking.

Less is more

There is no greater insult for a leader than to be accused of an absence of leadership at the top of the organization they are supposed to be running. Yet the bravest Humans are prepared to give it a go. Not an absence of leadership per se, but an absence of top-down leadership. The idea that less is more has caught on but the question remains how to implement it.

A Swedish consulting firm, Crisp, offers the most extreme example. It garnered much attention a few years ago for declaring it could run itself perfectly well without a leader. It is structured as a non-profit company for more than 35 independently minded IT consultants who prefer some of the support structure that an employee benefits from. They chip in fees every year to cover central costs but Crisp has no growth target and no ambition to build up financial value in the firm.

'If we keep the company lean, with only a small liquidity buffer, then we don't need to argue about who owns what,' it says on its website.[3] Therefore ownership, which is offered to anyone who has been with the firm for two years, is largely symbolic. Crisp's main purpose is to enable consultants to be happy and a staff happiness index is keenly watched. 'Strong revenue and delighted customers are a side effect, not a goal,' it added.

It sounds a little like a smaller, stripped-down version of Arup, the engineering firm featured in the Diplomats chapter, which distributes the majority of its surplus to 'members' every year. Swedish law demands that Crisp must have a board of directors, but anyone can attend board meetings. Decision making is not via a single well-defined process, because 'Different types of decisions need a different process. It would be crazy to involve the whole team in decisions like which type of whiteboard pens to buy. And it would be crazy to NOT involve the whole team if we needed to move our office to a new location.' The person driving an issue owns the decision process. In 2015, Crisp published its DNA – effectively an operating manual – open source, for anyone to replicate it for themselves.

Nick Pearson hasn't quite sacked himself but you suspect it might not be out of the question. As the unflashy chief executive of Parkrun, he oversees a very modern brand that powers 350,000 runners of all abilities on a timed five-kilometre run every Saturday morning – when Covid-19-enforced social distancing allows.

It is not a charity so much as a movement. Parkrun has a laudable mission: to be free forever and to support the least active communities. Its popularity sees to it that #parkrun trends on social media most Saturday mornings. And rather than adopting the elite sports target to go faster and faster, it prides itself that its average running time is going up as far-from-fit people give it a try.

Parkrun is also a wonderfully British institution that exists only because of legions of volunteers, in this case 35,000 people who show up every weekend to marshal the course and time the runners. Pearson, who took over running the charity from its founder in 2015, is clear about his place. It has much in common with a Diplomat. 'You definitely can't lead by memo, by directive or by too many rules,' he said in 2019. 'You lead them predominantly by vision, by culture, by championing what they are doing, by showing the world the positive impact they are having.'[4]

Parkrun began life as the Bushy Park Time Trial in Teddington, Middlesex, the leafy border of London. The founder Paul Sinton-Hewitt was a club runner who had just lost his job and was suffering from a leg injury. For his first event in October 2004, 13 entrants took part. A second regular event, on Wimbledon Common, was added in 2007. For a long time, Sinton-Hewitt funded the organization until a first sponsor was recruited in 2009. Eventually, he put Parkrun into a charitable trust.

Since then it has spread to 22 countries and amassed 7 million registered runners. The dedicated grass roots effort means that someone running in Soweto or San Francisco is guaranteed the same experience. Somehow it has stayed small at the centre, with an expected turnover of £7 million in 2020 and just 43 permanent members of staff.

Much of that is down to Pearson. He had previously been managing director of Sweatshop, an independent specialist sports retailer that had its own running initiative. His challenge at Parkrun was to create a workable model from a brilliant idea. With the mindset of one of the organization's participants he aimed for a sharp focus that stripped away any extraneous activity and kept money purposefully tight. Pearson wanted enough income to cover costs but didn't want to festoon each event with sponsors' messages which, because of Parkrun's popularity, he could easily have done.

'I think the future for almost all organizations is redefining what lean is and what productivity is,' this Human said. 'I think there is a lack of focus and therefore organizations built around things that they don't need to be doing and shouldn't be doing because they have lost what that focus is.'

Pearson added, '(I have to) make sure we are absolutely doing the maximum we can with the minimum level of resource and investment. That is how we will be sustainable for 10 and 20 years. We won't be sustainable if we build a model that needs to double in size every two-and-a-half years like our participation is (doing), because our costs will spiral and spiral.'

Forever embedded

The alternative to small-scale, consensual leadership as demonstrated by Parkrun is the Human who embeds themselves as much as possible in their organization. If they can't flatten the firm while maintaining effectiveness, they make sure they are closely in touch with the grass roots.

When he was elected as senior partner at the Magic Circle law firm Linklaters in 2016, Charlie Jacobs insisted on ringfencing half of his time to remain on client work. It was a fresh spin on the classic Diplomat leadership role, and has helped him stay better connected with day-to-day business than he might have done if he was purely the firm's figurehead.

The timing of his decision to stand for election was also notable. Jacobs, tall, trim and bespectacled, went for the job at the relatively young age of 49 – perhaps five years sooner than bosses typically did. 'There was a lot going on in the legal industry and I thought I could still run at a very fast pace,' he said in 2019. 'I think if you take it on too late, the danger is you take it on as a pipe and slippers, retirement job.'

Born in Cape Town to a South African father and an Irish mother, Jacobs followed his two older sisters to the UK to study, having been advised by his father that the post-Big Bang London could be a better place to start his career than under the uncertain apartheid regime. At Linklaters first as a vacation student in 1988, he was a rare non-Oxbridge recruit, which lent him an outsider perspective that has proved useful. Jacobs rose to fame on the back of block-buster deals such as AB InBev's 2015 $100 billion takeover of SABMiller, which redrew the map of the brewing industry, and the 2012 merger of commodities giant Glencore with miner Xstrata.

As leader, he worked hard to make the role work for him by not being hidebound by what had gone before. Law firms are guilty of demanding that their staff remain connected at all times. Jacobs the Human wanted to see people face-to-face where possible, not just at the other end of an iPhone message or Zoom call. Whenever he arrived in one of Linklaters' 30 offices around the world, he headed to the gym, not the boardroom, to find out what was going on. He was no fan of after-hours drinks and preferred a pre-work spinning class that allowed him to mingle with colleagues from all levels while working up a sweat. 'I get a different cross-section of people coming, we get a shake or a fruit juice afterwards and they can see a more down-to-earth side to the senior partner,' he said.

He also tried to break down the traditional sense of how a law firm operates. The industry will never truly reform workplace culture unless it can divorce itself from the model of billable hours. Charging an annual 2,000 hours of their time out to clients has long been an article of faith impressed on new recruits. Jacobs tried to get colleagues to see past the numbers game because profits are shared among partners in lockstep with each other. There are unwelcome reminders that his profession is well paid but also tough. Paul Rawlinson, the chair of another major law firm, Baker McKenzie, died in early 2019, six months after taking a leave of absence, citing exhaustion.

'We said we're going to de-emphasize the individual metrics,' Jacobs said. 'We want people to think firm first, practice second, individual third. I don't care what your individual numbers are. I'm going to sit down with you once a year and say who are your clients, what have you worked on in the previous year and what do people think of you internally and externally? In a lockstep environment, that's all I need to know.' Jacobs the always-on dealmaker might have resisted such a move when he was bringing in many millions of pounds of business. He agreed. 'I would have been one of the ones a little bit cynical to start, but I would have given it a go.' The introduction of sober chaperones to oversee drinks parties that in the past risked getting out of hand plays further to the staff welfare theme.

Humans are sure that doing better for their people makes for a better business. Clare Gilmartin, chief executive of European rail ticketing app Trainline since 2014, has first-hand experience of being given a little extra leeway to juggle her work and home life.

Returning to work at eBay earlier in her career after having her first two children, she needed time to readjust. That meant dropping back to a four-day week for six months.

'We need to encourage people to ask for more flexibility; not forever, just for a certain phase,' she said in a 2016 interview. 'Boy, do I think it pays off. If you can help women and men manage through challenging points in their career, they will be super-loyal and thrive thereafter.'[5]

Gilmartin is among a crop of leaders who understand that their company's talent is a resource, not just a cost centre – and they are active in nurturing it. Enlightened Humans have been active in pushing the focus on mental health in the workplace up the agenda. In addition, greater awareness of LBGTQ+ issues encourages staff to bring their whole selves to the office so they feel liberated and able to produce their best work.

One direction

Whatever leadership type, direction must still be set from the top. Humans take perhaps the broadest view of what that direction should be and how it is decided upon.

Peter Jackson, the chief executive since 2018 of Flutter Entertainment, the FTSE 100 online gambling group whose brands include Paddy Power, Betfair, Fanduel and TVG, summed up his responsibility as threefold: to set the company's direction, communicate that direction to everyone, and make sure he employed the best people, who were looked after well. Flutter handles more than 3 billion punters' transactions a year and has plans to grow. In October 2019 it announced a proposed merger with the Stars Group which brings PokerStars, Full Tilt and Sky Bet into its portfolio. The industry had been racing to expand in the United States as online gambling was gradually legalized.

'I have learnt over time that great people don't want to be told what to do,' said Jackson. 'People call it micro management, whatever, I prefer to call it being a dictator and no one wants to work for a dictator. You need to give great people empowerment. If they know where they are going, they are going to get there.'[6]

Nor is he going to formulate strategy from the top. 'There are 8,000 colleagues across the organization. Am I going to be the source of good ideas in the business? Absolutely no way. There are 7,999 people who have got much more experience in our space than I have. That is why I do see it as my role to make sure that I am creating the right supportive environment for them... to encourage and reward and incentivize.'

Jackson, who previously led foreign exchange company Travelex and Worldpay UK, the payment processing firm, resisted tinkering with the company plan if he could help it. In fact, collectivism was more important to him than perfection.

'Ultimately, clever people can try to fiddle with things too much; it can be tempting to tweak and change the strategy because it is intellectually rewarding but actually it is not helpful. What is much more important is that people have clarity around where we are going. Actually, heading slightly in the wrong direction but having the whole organization heading there is much better than having people partially headed in one direction and then changing it six months later.'

Conclusion

The quest to improve the discipline of leadership is ongoing. That it needs a revamp suggests something is inherently wrong with the way in which companies are organized and directed.

The creeping suspicion that capitalism and its captains are failing is aroused every time a new financial black hole is discovered; whenever the latest collapse or cover-up is exposed. Certainly, corporate leaders have yet to solve the problem of wealth inequality, pointed at as proof that the entire financial system could do better.

Yet leadership does not simply benefit from continuous improvement like the fine-tuning of a factory production line. The metrics which determine its success have multiplied in a generation like the shift from analogue to digital technology.

The Humans cited in this chapter are well aware of the numerous targets they must hit, from the sustainable, shared gains of profit, to well-being, enjoyment and minimal environmental harm.

They operate with shareholders in mind, but also with the shop worker or supplier on their shoulder reminding them how things are in the real world beyond the boardroom. They strive to be as inclusive and authentic as possible. Their true power is as an enabling force for others.

And if they get it wrong they learn quickly from their mistakes. The best leaders are open to change and renewal.

HUMANS IN BRIEF

Strengths: Risk taking, deep thinking, closeness to workforce, closeness to society, authenticity, transparency.

Weaknesses: At times too experimental and thinly spread.

Suitability: For the future.
Where you will find them: Coming to a business near
you – if they haven't arrived already.

Endnotes

This chapter: original Isabelle Kocher, Zhang Ruimin, Charlie Jacobs
interviews

1 Drucker, P (nd) 'The best way to predict your future is to create
   it' – lessons for today's leaders from the creative writing process. https://
   www.druckerchallenge.org/uploads/pics/Prem_Kumar_Drucker
   Challenge_Submission_PK_120446965.pdf (archived at https://perma.
   cc/UK45-MLT9)

2 Mallet, B and Rose, M (2020) French energy group Engie ousts CEO
   Isabelle Kocher, *Reuters*, 6 February. https://www.reuters.com/article/
   engie-kocher-board/refile-update-3-french-energy-group-engie-ousts-ceo-
   isabelle-kocher-idUSL8N2A67AM (archived at https://perma.cc/
   UK45-MLT9)

3 Crisp DNA (nd) The inner workings of a rather different consulting
   company. https://dna.crisp.se/docs/ (archived at https://perma.cc/7TMT-
   QRPT)

4 Ashton, J (2019) Leading with James Ashton Episode 9 – Wellcome Trust
   and Parkrun, *Apple Podcasts*, 2 July. https://podcasts.apple.com/gb/podcast/
   episode-9-wellcome-trust-and-parkrun/id1460796936?i=1000443414458
   (archived at https://perma.cc/9TXK-75DD)

5 Ashton, J (2016) Striking the ideal work-life balance that keeps
   Trainline's boss on track, *The Times*, 25 November. https://www.
   thetimes.co.uk/article/striking-the-ideal-work-life-balance-that-keeps-
   trainlines-boss-on-track-rqr20xgj3 (archived at https://perma.cc/
   QYR7-VYXQ)

6 Ashton, J (2019) Leading with James Ashton Episode 7 – Flutter
   Entertainment and Fairtrade, *Apple Podcasts*, 10 June. https://podcasts.
   apple.com/gb/podcast/episode-7-flutter-entertainment-and-fairtrade/
   id1460796936?i=1000441048389 (archived at https://perma.cc/
   CPZ7-QTWX)

Epilogue

The latter stages of this book were written during the acutest test of leadership in living memory. While I tapped away to bring *The Nine Types of Leader* to life locked down in Surrey, chief executives – many of them in the unfamiliar confinement of home offices – were blending emergency protocols with all they had learnt in their careers thus far to pull their company and colleagues along.

Many of them I spoke to were doubtful that Covid-19 would change everything in the long term. By summer, in trading updates scored with red ink that counted the cost of coronavirus, the desire to get back on track was obvious. But as corporations steadied themselves, with any sense of normality regarded a victory, it was clear that few bosses were likely to let a good crisis go to waste.

Covid-19 will do for leadership what it has done to all aspects of society: perhaps not introduce new trends but certainly speed up the spread of behaviours that were already emerging. For consumers that means more home deliveries, timeshifted TV, video calling with grandma, the simple pleasure of sitting in the garden and re-evaluating the vital contribution of public sector workers.

In a corporate setting, the virus will be a huge accelerant for cost-cutting, flattening, digitizing, working remotely, laying waste to firms that were struggling anyway and birthing numerous start-ups. For business leaders, it means three things.

First, a global recession means a period of grinding sales and lower returns in which investors will have less patience with weak businesses and weak leaders. It is a reminder that the profit imperative, while not a sole driver of corporate success, remains at its heart and a licence for all else.

Second, the pandemic has reasserted the social contract between business and society. Companies that needed state support largely received it and those firms that could help those in need did so without question. For a fleeting moment, we were all in it together. Businesses and their leaders will fail their customers and staff if they forget they are part of a wider community.

And third, workforces will be more dispersed than ever. Remote working stands to shave millions from a company's property costs, but it means leaders must become more adept at projecting their message from afar. With fewer touchpoints and town hall meetings, they must think hard how to use technology to build teams, enable others to prosper and oversee quality control, productivity, morale and staff well-being.

In more than two decades of meeting and interviewing business leaders, I know that change is a constant – changing faces, changing technologies, changing styles.

What will never change is that the best leaders combine purpose, authenticity and delivery. They have the broadest vision and the ability to inspire those around them. And that compels people to follow them somewhere no one has ever been: the future.

Index